Chinese Cooking
for
American Kitchens

Chinese Cooking for American Kitchens

CALVIN LEE

With Illustrations by Mabel Wong Lilienstein

641.59
L 477
49474

G. P. P̶u̶t̶n̶a̶m̶'̶s̶ ̶S̶o̶n̶s̶ NEW YORK

Published in the Dominion of Canada by
Longmans, Green & Company, Toronto.

Second Impression

Library of Congress Catalog Card Number: 58-7448

Manufactured in the United States of America

TO UNCLE TERRY

Acknowledgments:

I am grateful to Terry Ho for helping to translate Lee's Restaurant recipes into easily workable recipes for the home, to my wife Beverly who let me monopolize her kitchen for months and typed the recipes, and to David Edwards for assisting with historical research.

Contents

Foreword

It's useless for me to try to speak unemotionally about Calvin Lee. In the first place he's my godson. I picked him myself. In the second place, I admire extravagantly his courage, determination and filial feeling, having watched his struggle since his father's death to support his mother, his young brother and sister, and at the same time put himself through law school.

I fell in love one night at dinner with the Lees; first with sweet and sour pork, then with George Lee. He was a quiet man of great integrity, who literally worked himself to death to maintain the good business his father had started in Chinatown. Thus at the age of forty-two, George, who never spent less than eighteen hours a day at the restaurant, died. Calvin was seventeen, Bo Lummy was twelve and Lilly was eight. Overnight Calvin became the head of the house, and against the protests of all his kin determined to finish college and carry on the restaurant at the same time.

The mother, Wei, knew that her husband's dying wish had

11

been that no child of his should have to forgo an education to keep up the business. For the first time, she began to work actively in the restaurant, learned to be a cashier, took lessons in English. She still cannot pronounce most of the names of her customers, but she knows them all—the man who is always arguing with his wife, the one who eats lychee nuts, the couple who have ghosts in their house, the long-winded woman. She does not know most of the customers by sight, for she insists that "all Caucasians look alike." Everybody loves to see her darting about in her bright Chinese robes, always smiling, always gracious and concerned for the diner's comfort.

Calvin has finished law school now and is a practicing lawyer, Bo Lum will soon be graduated from college, and Lilly will begin her four years. Then Wei will feel that George Lee's dreams have been accomplished.

MARY MARGARET McBRIDE

Preface

Mary Margaret McBride boasts a little that she is godmother to the author, but I am godmother to this book.

Often with a slight touch of bitterness Calvin Lee recalls that it was I who first got him "mixed up with food."

At that time, soon after the death of his father, Calvin was at Columbia and planning to study dentistry. I was doing a radio program on food and restaurants. And Estella Karn, Mary Margaret's manager and Best Friend to us all, acting in her usual role as perennial bringer-together, introduced my husband, Walter White, and me to the Lee family and their restaurant.

It was Stella's idea that Calvin might make a good guest for my program and the publicity could do the restaurant no harm.

Calvin was filially affectionate to Stella, a co-godmother with Mary Margaret. He was charmingly polite to me and completely entranced by Walter White with whom he proceeded to settle world problems in depth and breadth. It was

13

in many ways a memorable occasion. As of that evening, Calvin decided to desert dentistry and devote himself to the world of Walter White, the law and international relations.

Every so often Stella and I pierced the enchanted circle and brought up the subject of food and the radio program.

Patiently, Calvin tried to explain that although by a series of circumstances which included his father and his grandfather before him, he had been catapulted into the restaurant business, he knew nothing about Chinese food and cared, if possible, less.

Nevertheless, in order to please his godmothers and his new-found idol, Walter White, he did consent to bone up with Uncle Terry who was his uncle and mentor in everything but actual fact. A week or two later, primed with all manner of interesting fact, lore and even recipes, he did make his first—highly successful—radio appearance.

The word gets around. Within a year or two Calvin Lee had become the unofficial spokesman of Chinatown. Every radio and television commentator in town had him on the program. Especially during the Chinese New Year season, Calvin bounded like a movie star, from interview to interview.

As time went on he showed slightly more interest in gastronomic matters. In fact, once or twice, he even introduced the subject into the conversation. But he was, if possible, even more surprised than I when the idea of doing a cookbook was broached to him.

Although I know that Calvin Lee is a demon for work and a dogged genius for research; although I had seen the red-bound book of his ancestral recipes; although I knew of the endless conversations that had been conducted over a period of many months with Uncle Terry, and the testing and retesting that had been done by Calvin himself and by his mother and Beverly, his bride; nevertheless, I approached the manuscript not knowing and maybe a little afraid.

Hallelujah is the only word! This is the best, the most basic, the most analytical and the most practical Chinese cookbook I have ever seen.

Nowhere else is there such a description of a Chinese grocery store—a wonderland for the adventurous epicure, but a wonderland where it was, before this book, all too easy to be lost.

Calvin Lee lists the various meats and vegetables, the sauces and seasonings which you can find in Chinatown. He suggests, whenever possible, American substitutes and lists the recipes that call for special ingredients.

The chapter on bringing China into your home, the description of Chinese cooking utensils and their American equivalent should prove invaluable.

Even those who never cook but only eat will find delight and utility in the chapter which makes clear in the simplest terms the mysteries of the Chinese menu; how to order in a Chinese restaurant; how to know by learning just half a dozen words exactly what you are about to receive.

More than anything else I am enthralled by the last chapter on tea. Calvin Lee introduced me a long time ago to a tea of chrysanthemum flowers which he says is to be "mixed with rock candy and drunk with Chinese pastry after meals." I have tasted already the Jasmine of Taiwan, "for reading poetry with your love." Now, I shall not rest until I have known tea plucked by monkeys in the highest mountains and the Eyebrows of Longevity, a green tea of Canton, "served in the garden on a spring afternoon."

POPPY CANNON

1. Chinese Food and Culture

The Chinese have a kitchen god, Joh-quon. The picture of Joh-quon is situated on the top of the hearth of every kitchen and he, being the only god who has spent every moment of the year in the house, is able to report to heaven all the goings on in the household. At the end of each year all the gods are summoned to the "Jade Emperor" in heaven to make a report on their activities. Since the kitchen god keeps an account of the family, a bad report to heaven may result in the loss of the little wealth the family has or bad health for one of the family. In order to make sure that the report is good, the kitchen god is given a farewell dinner on the night of the twenty-fourth day of the twelfth month. The dinner consists only of sweet things so that he can only say sweet words when reporting. His mouth is rubbed with honey and he is offered cakes, candied fruits and sweet rice dishes. All this is sheer bribery and it is commonly known that he will accept the bribe. After the dinner the image of

17

the kitchen god is seated upon some bamboo stalks with a horse made of paper. With the murmur of some prayer the kitchen god, the paper horse, and the bamboo stalks are set afire and sent to heaven.

Cooking in China is an art that appears in the earliest literature of the country. According to one legend, Huang-Ti, who lived about 4,000 years ago, was the founder of the art and science of zestful cookery.

There is another legend that the Emperor Chien Lung of the Manchu dynasty was touring through Hangchow when he stopped at a peasant's food stand and asked the peasant to serve him lunch. The poor frightened peasant put together the few meager ingredients which he had and served the dish to the emperor, who enjoyed it so much that he asked what it was called. The peasant, not wanting the lord to know what was actually in the dish, called it "red-beaked green parrot with gold-trimmed jade cake." After the emperor had executed several palace chefs because they could not reproduce this dish by cooking a parrot with a piece of valuable jade, the peasant was finally summoned to the palace where he confessed that the dish which was served to the emperor was actually spinach with crimson roots and fried bean curd.

The Chinese philosophers and scholars such as Yuan Mei and Li Luweng took great delight in writing about food. Yuan Mei in one of his books gives his advice on eating:

Don't eat with your ears! By this I mean, do not plan a conglomeration of expensive, out-of-the-way dishes just to give your guests something to talk about. For that is to eat with the ears, not with the mouth. Bean curd, if good, is actually better than bird's nest.

Don't eat with your eyes! By this I mean, do not cover the table with innumerable dishes and an indefinite variety of courses. For this is to eat with the eyes and not with the mouth.

Hundreds of dos and don'ts in eating have persisted through the ages in China and no one seems to know the sources of them. Some seem reasonable whereas others are completely baffling. "Rice should be taken warm, soups hot, sauces cool, and drinks cold. In the selection of flavors, sour is good in spring, bitter in summer, pungent in autumn, and salt in winter."

There are hundreds of styles of cooking in China. Most foreigners assume that Chinese food is simply Chinese food but they could not be more mistaken. It is true, however, that almost all of the Chinese cooking in America is Cantonese and therefore most people are misled into thinking that there is only this one style of Chinese cooking. In large cities such as New York there are restaurants which cater to the Mandarin, Shanghai, or Northern taste. Many Chinese cookbooks which have been published in this country have been written by people who cook Northern-style and not Cantonese-style. To her dismay, the cook cannot understand why the recipe never comes out the same as the way it is prepared in the Cantonese restaurant nearby.

Since China is so very large, it is not surprising that there are such differences there in taste of food. The difference in produce in each part of the country naturally makes a difference in the cuisine. And even aside from the varied geography of the country, the people from the various sectors have different temperaments and even speak different dialects, so different that a person from one village may not be able to understand someone from another village even if they live only 50 miles from each other.

In spite of this confusion, all the various styles and forms of cooking can be grouped into five schools: Canton, Fukien, Honan, Shantung, and Szechuen. Cantonese cooking is the most popular even in China itself. There is a saying, "To be born in Soo Chow, to eat in Kwang Chow [i.e. Canton], to dress in Hang Chow, and to die in Leou Chow." For Soo Chow is known for beauty, Canton for food, Hang Chow for silk, and Leou Chow for the wood which coffins are made of.

Although each of these five schools of Chinese cooking uses almost the same basic ingredients, such as black mushrooms, bamboo shoots and soy sauce, there is a difference in the taste of their foods.

Shantung, the native land of Confucius and Mencius, probably acquired its interest in food through the influence of these sages. Its dishes are light and surprisingly there are hardly any *chow* or what we call stir-fried dishes which are so popular in Cantonese food and among Americans. Shantung is known for its wine-cooked meats and soft fried dishes and the Peking duck. Peking, by the way, has no school of its own but adopts the Shantung school. It is therefore incorrect to say that a certain restaurant serves food in the Peking style, although many restaurants do advertise that they have Peking cooking.

Fukien probably produces the best soy sauce in China. Because of its long seacoast this area is especially well known for its seafood. The Fukienese are especially fond of soup and soupy dishes, so much so that a fourth of all the dishes at a Fukien banquet may be soups. There is a saying that if you have dinner at the home of a Fukienese and he does not serve you at least two soups, you may assume that he does not like you. The food is very light and the soups are generally very clear.

The food of the Honan school is richer than that of Fukien but here again there is not the variety and splendor of Cantonese cooking. Honanese are fond of spicy foods, hot dishes, and sweet and sours, for which they are particularly known. It may well be that sweet and sour spare ribs (Tiem shuen pei quot), so very popular in Chinese restaurants in America, came originally from Honan. The pride and joy of Honan is its delicacy bear's paw, something which most Cantonese and Americans are not too eager to try.

The food of Szechuen is inclined to be oily and hot-tasting. Hot pepper is used freely during the preparation of the food or before serving. This area has not taken full advantage of its rich soil and variable climate so far as its cooking goes.

Yang Chow, although it is not important enough to form a school of cooking, has made its impact especially in America because it originated fried rice (chow fon). Fried rice as contrasted to chop suey, which was originated in America, is an authentic Chinese dish and for many years was always called Yang Chow Fried Rice.

Because of its greater variety of seafood and vegetables, Cantonese cooking has a greater number of dishes than any other school. Americans are most familiar with little-oil stir-fried (chow) dishes, which make up about 90 per cent of the menu in most restaurants. This method of cooking, described in Chapter IV, preserves the texture and flavor of the meat and vegetables. Cantonese cooking is more international in taste than any of the other schools of Chinese cooking. It does not depend on any hot or unusual spices, though it makes full use of soy sauce and fresh ginger root. It can also be adapted to any meats or vegetables which you have on hand. Besides being famous for stir-fry dishes, Canton is also known for shark's fin soup, bird's nest soup, and steamed delicacies such as shrimp dumplings (Har gow) and steamed meat patties (Shu mei). Anyone interested in Chinese cooking should become familiar with steamed Cantonese dishes such as steamed bass with black bean sauce (Jing yu), steamed beef with salted cabbage (Chung choy jing ngow), and steamed ground pork with salted egg (Hom don jing gee yok).

The great popularity of Chinese food in America has often overshadowed the other influences of Chinese culture on Western civilization, in art, literature, and design. Even before the Chinese arrived in America their culture was felt during the rococo style which came to the United States indirectly from Europe. Although trade relations between Europe and the Orient were firmly established in the sixteenth and seventeenth centuries, it was not until the eighteenth century that Chinese culture made a major impact on Western Europe. In 1687 the Confucian Classics were translated into French, leading writers of the Enlightenment such as Voltaire, Rousseau and Lebrun to depict China as an ideal society based on natural law with a philosopher king at its head. In the philosophical conflict between naturalism and revealed religion, the example of China as a thriving civilization without benefit of Christianity was used as evidence that the deity could be found through natural order without revelation.

The philosophical idealization of China led to the great popularity of everything Chinese. Chinese painting, porcelains, lacquers, embroideries, wallpapers and curios were imported in great amounts. These were imitated and became the *chinoiseries* of the shell-like rococo art of the period. This decorative fad spread throughout Europe. Maria Theresa of Austria added a "Chinese apartment" to her palace at Schönbrunn to house Chinese curios, Frederick the Great of Prussia built an oriental pavilion at Sans Souci; and the Elector of Bavaria constructed a pagoda. Soon architecture picked up the Chinese interior and its round corner, aptly calling it the Chinese corner. Gardens were designed in what was imagined to be the Chinese manner. At the height of the fad New Year's Day was celebrated at the French court with Chinese food, costumes, and entertainment.

Works with a "Chinese" touch were expected of the European artists and craftsmen. In painting, Watteau led a movement which departed from the stylization of the classical period to a style possessing a suggestion of Chinese form and feeling. This impressionistic treatment of nature in their pastoral scenes was an innovation in Western art which became an essential element in the transition from classicism to romanticism.

The mid-eighteenth-century enthusiasm for *chinoiserie* decoration was reflected in the blue and white (Delft) porcelain of Holland. In England, Thomas Chippendale adapted Chinese furniture designs in dark mahoganies which became world-famous. It was inevitable that this craze should reach the American colonies. Chinese objects, particularly fine wallpapers, played an important role in interior decoration. These can be seen today at the restorations at Williamsburg and Winterthur in Delaware as well as in many museum rooms throughout the country. In Philadelphia, especially, the style had a definite effect on architecture. The first direct contact between the United States and China was in 1784. On February 22 of that year, one month after the proclamation of peace with Great Britain, a small merchantman, the *Empress of China,* left New York harbor with the first cargo of goods for trade with China. With this ship's successful return, the China trade which would culminate in the era of the clipper ships in 1850 had begun.

As the trade with China increased, the first group of Chinese immigrants arrived in the United States. Unlike other immigrants, the Chinese looked upon the absence from their native land as only a temporary excursion among the white barbarians caused by economic or political adversity at home. The major emigration from China occurred soon after the Gold Rush of '49. The Chinese today still call this country Gum San (Gold Mountain). The rush of emigration was increased by the disturbed political conditions of the southern provinces. The Triad Society, a secret order opposed to the Manchu dynasty, seized upon the time when the government was busy combating the Tai Ping rebellion in the north to start an insurrection. This was crushed with much bloodshed and thousands of the rebels sought refuge in America with many others who were ruined by the uprising. Thus among the immigrants were a number of intellectuals and revolutionists who were forced by circumstances to work as common laborers when they arrived in this country.

Most of the Chinese worked on the Union Pacific Railroad, strawberry farms, in cigar factories or mills. But under the illusion that the Chinese would flood the labor market, a peak of anti-Chinese feeling was reached as early as 1876. Anti-Chinese mass meetings and lynchings were held all over California. The culmination of these feelings finally brought about the Chinese Exclusion Bill of 1884, which precluded the immigration of Chinese laborers. This bill was extended until 1945 at which time a fantastically low quota of 105 persons per year was set for a nation which has a population of 500 million.

For the Chinese who stayed in America after the Union Pacific was built, life was not easy at all. Bills were passed against Chinese immigration and attempts were made to ship all the Chinese back to China. They did not speak English and it was said that they would never fit into American society. By living together in small areas which later grew into Chinatowns, these people found that they could get along without having to adjust to the American way of living. The Chinatowns had their own form of law enforcement and trade regulations; they were almost completely self-supporting.

The movement of Chinese into the laundry and restaurant business in America was a natural one. The completion of the Union Pacific Railroad threw thousands of Chinese out of work. They sought other employment and many soon found that the laundry business was a remunerative one. It is said that a Mr. Thomas of New Jersey hired 50 Chinese to work in his laundry in 1869. When they got there, they discovered the great demand for this type of work and the news not only spread to the West Coast but back to China as well. Thousands of Chinese came east until there was scarcely a town which did not have a Chinese hand laundry.

Little restaurants grew in the towns where there were a number of Chinese homesick for their native cuisine. Some of their chefs were probably cooks for the work gangs of the Union Pacific, some were domestic servants for white families, a few were trained chefs from the old country who were imported here especially for the purpose of the restaurant business. One of these chefs who was trained in China was my grandfather, Hung Lee, who opened his restaurant in New York's Chinatown back in 1892. Most of the recipes in this book are adapted from his secret recipes which were written into a little rice-paper notebook and handed down to my father and to my own generation.

2. Chinese Food Comes to America

There are several versions of the story of how chop suey originated in America. According to one, some hungry miners in San Francisco were looking for a place to eat late one night. All the restaurants were closed except for a Chinese restaurant where only Chinese ate. At this time few Americans had ever had the courage or foresight to try Chinese food. The miners demanded to be fed, and the chef took what was left over, put it together with sauces and served it. The hungry miners enjoyed the meal so much that they wanted to know what the dish was called. The only name which the chef could give the leftovers was "chop suey" which means hash. The miners came back for more and the news spread and soon all Chinese restaurants served chop suey for Americans.

The other story of the origin of chop suey is told about His Excellency Li Hung-Chang, the premier of China who visited this country on a good-will tour in 1896. Many banquets and receptions were given in his honor and in order to reciprocate he brought his own chef to entertain his hosts. But the premier being a wise man wasn't sure that his guests would enjoy such Chinese delicacies as bird's nest, shark's fin, bear's paw and others. He therefore had his chef prepare American meats and vegetables in the Chinese manner with the appropriate sauces and chopping. He named it "chop suey" because it was a combination of chopped mixed foods.

Once Americans were introduced to Chinese cooking, even though it was only Chinese-style American food in the beginning, they kept coming back for more and so created a greater and greater demand for Chinese food. The more adventurous Americans went down to the Chinatowns and ate at the restaurants which only the Chinese had patronized. Authentic dishes became popular.

One of the early peaks in the Chinese restaurant business was reached in the early twenties, coinciding with the Mah Jong craze. Two brothers named White had introduced the game with simplified rules to the English-speaking clubs in Shanghai, where it became popular. The game met with such success in America that by 1923 the Chinese makers of Mah Jong sets could no longer keep up with the demand and American manufacture was in full swing. A Mah Jong League of America was formed.

The Roaring Twenties and the age of prohibition brought with it dozens of huge, magnificent Chinese restaurants with dance floors and entertainment. In the larger cities where night-clubbing was prevalent, it became a fad to eat down in Chinatown at some wee hour in the morning after a whole evening of night-clubbing. The Chinese restaurants were among the few open at this time of night. It was a romantic idea to wander through the little streets of Chinatown at some unearthly hour and then sober up with fine Chinese food.

In the "Chop Suey Era" only chop suey, chow mein, fried rice and egg foo young were popular. Many Chinese restaurants in small towns still confine their menus to these few dishes. World War II marked the beginning of a wider interest in Chinese food in America. It is difficult to pinpoint the cause of this growing interest but it may have been that Chinese cooking was especially adapted to the meat rationing situation during the war. As you will see in the recipes later in the book, a Chinese dish requires only about one quarter the amount of meat which a normal American dish may require. Even today, without meat rationing, Chinese cooking is popular because it is so economical. The dishes which became most famous at this time are lobster Cantonese (Chow lung har), shrimp with lobster sauce, Moo goo gai peen, (chicken with mushrooms), barbecue spare ribs and wonton soup.

Today, although Chinese food is still considered to be fascinating, unusual and romantic, it has become a habit and a regular diet for many Americans. They no longer eat just chop suey and chow mein but have expanded their diets to Niw goo yok (sweet and sour pork—a dish which my godmother Mary Margaret McBride made famous), Wor shew opp (braised boneless duck topped with crushed almonds), Char shu ding (diced roast pork with mushrooms and assorted vegetables sprinkled with toasted almonds) and many others which are included in this book. Some say that this great interest in the exotic dishes was stimulated by soldiers who were stationed in the Far East and had tasted the "real thing." Regardless of whether it should be attributed to these veterans or whether it was just a natural outgrowth of an already growing desire to learn more about the food, we have finally reached the day when Chinese food is a part of American everyday living.

The last step which will complete the development of Chinese food in America is taking place today. That, of course, is the serving of Chinese food in American homes.

In New York the first Chinese restaurants were started right in Chinatown exclusively for the Chinese trade. Most of my grandfather's patrons were homesick Chinese sailors and merchants. Our family business was called "Uie Ye Kwen"; literally translated it means "at your pleasure." (Incidentally the name Uie Ye Kwen was changed to Lee's Restaurant by my father in 1932 because no American could ever pronounce the name correctly.) The dining room consisted simply of round wooden-top tables and little round stools with wooden shelves on all the walls for all sorts of ingredients. My grandfather was the chef, dishwasher, cashier, waiter, and everything else. Lee's Restaurant was among the first restaurants in New York to have a Caucasian trade. A photograph of the restaurant in 1900 shows a large sign outside the door with the words: *Caucasian Trade Welcome.*

The story of the Lee family is what one might call an American story. It is the story of an immigrant, his son and his grandchildren, and their lives in America. New York is called the melting pot of the world, but somehow things don't melt so easily when your physical features are different from the majority of the people and also when you have thousands of years of culture behind you. My father, George

Lee, who was born in New York, was a good example of the second-generation Chinese-American. In the typical old-fashioned custom, he was sent to China while he was young to learn how to read and write Chinese and also how to cook so that he could take over the business when the time came. It is in the second-generation Americans, like my father, that one really sees the blending of culture. When he took over the restaurant in 1932 he completely remodeled the interior so that it became one of the first modern Chinese restaurants in New York. The food and recipes were never changed although some names of dishes were Anglicized to make it easier for the American customer to order a meal. With this bit of combining the oriental cooking with American business acumen, my father built the little Chinese food shop into a nationally known restaurant. There were many men like my father who were responsible for making Chinese food a part of the American diet.

If the second-generation Chinese-Americans were responsible for building up the interest in Chinese restaurants and Chinese food, the third and future generations may be responsible for letting this interest lie fallow unless new Chinese immigrants come into this country. Chinese-Americans who are third-generation Americans like myself are in a strange predicament. We were brought up in fairly modern homes, not much different from that of any other American family. My father and I used to go to the Yankee games, the Bronx zoo, and the circus and then top things off with a steak dinner somewhere in the city. But in some ways we were very Chinese. We spoke only Chinese at home and were taught all sorts of Chinese courtesies and manners. But the desire for emancipation from the group which has been dubbed as restaurantmen and laundrymen brings the culture of the parental group into contempt. The Chinese-Americans consider themselves Americans, no different from the way the Irish-Americans or Italian-Americans feel, and they are desirous of acquiring status in this group. They feel that such recognition will be more likely to come if they separate themselves from their racial group and they are willing to make sacrifices to bring this about. A number of Caucasians in this country, unfortunately, still do not distinguish these persons of American birth from their elders and consider them all unassimilable aliens.

The growth of the second and third generation of Chinese-Americans has brought about a change in the cooking and eating habits of Chinese mothers. Since most of our mothers were born and raised in China, it is somewhat surprising to see their adaptation to American food. Our friends often ask us, "What do you eat for breakfast at home?" So far as breakfast is concerned, we eat everything which every other American family eats. We have eggs, ham, bacon, oatmeal, toast, muffins, and all sorts of "crackling" and "popping" breakfast foods. As a matter of fact the children in Chinatown probably collect as many box tops as children in any other community. We used to send for everything that was offered on the radio such as the Lone Ranger rings, Captain Midnight secret codes, Captain Marvel club, and as a consequence had to finish boxes and boxes of breakfast foods.

Mothers in Chinatown, although they will not eat a sandwich for lunch themselves, get into the habit of packing sandwiches for their school children. There were times when our sandwiches were not the ordinary ham and cheese or roast beef sandwiches our classmates ate but were filled instead with lop chong (steamed Chinese pork sausage), char shu (roast pork) or beef prepared with soy sauce. Our mothers still do not "go" for American foods such as casseroles, meat loaves, salads, southern fried chicken or pork chops. When forced to order something in an American restaurant, they usually order steak and then complain how tasteless the Americans prepare their steaks. When steak is prepared in a Chinese home it is usually cooked with the vegetables so that the vegetables will absorb the juices of the meat and nothing is lost from its taste.

STEAK À LA LEE

1 pound sirloin steak
1½ tablespoons oil
1½ teaspoons salt
1 diced tomato
½ diced heart of celery
¼ cup sliced onions
1 cup sliced lettuce
½ cup water
¼ cup catsup

2 tablespoons Worcestershire sauce
2 teaspoons sugar
1 teaspoon monosodium glutamate
dash of pepper
2 teaspoons cornstarch mixed with 3 tablespoons water

Using a high flame, heat a frying pan with ½ tablespoon oil and ½ teaspoon salt. Fry steak for 2 minutes on each side. Remove and cut into 1-inch squares. Heat pan again with 1 tablespoon oil and 1 teaspoon salt. Add tomato, heart of celery, onions and lettuce and stir-fry for 2 minutes. Add water. Cover and cook for 1 minute. Add steak. Cover and cook for 1 minute. Add catsup, Worcestershire sauce, sugar, monosodium glutamate and pepper and cornstarch paste. Cook and stir for ½ minute.

Another more usual Chinese variation of steak is Steak Kow. You must remember that if the pan is not hot enough, the beef will become tough.

STEAK KOW

1 pound sirloin steak	¼ cup snow pea pods
1½ tablespoons oil	½ cup water
1½ teaspoons salt	1 tablespoon oyster sauce
1½ cups sliced Chinese celery cabbage (bok choy)	½ teaspoon sugar
¼ cup sliced water chestnuts	1 teaspoon monosodium glutamate
¼ cup sliced bamboo shoots	dash of pepper
¼ cup Chinese mushrooms (dung goo)	1 teaspoon cornstarch mixed with 2 tablespoons water

Soak mushrooms in cold water for ½ hour to soften. Drain and slice. Using a high flame, heat frying pan with ½ tablespoon oil and ½ teaspoon salt. Fry steak for 2 minutes on each side. Remove and cut into 1-inch squares. Heat pan again with 1 tablespoon oil and 1 teaspoon salt. Add celery cabbage, water chestnuts, bamboo shoots, mushrooms and snow pea pods and stir-fry for 2 minutes. Add water. Cover and cook for 2 minutes. Add steak. Cover and cook for 1 minute. Add oyster sauce, sugar, monosodium glutamate, pepper and cornstarch paste and cook and stir for ½ minute.

Pork chops can definitely be made much more delicious by using the Chinese-American recipe. For those who do not relish these recipes for Chinese steak, perhaps you will try this one on pork chops.

PORK CHOPS À LA LEE

3 pork chops
1½ tablespoons oil
1½ teaspoons salt
1 diced tomato
½ sliced heart of celery
¼ cup sliced onions
1 cup sliced lettuce
½ cup water
¼ cup catsup

2 tablespoons Worcestershire sauce
2 teaspoons sugar
1 teaspoon monosodium glutamate
dash of pepper
2 teaspoons cornstarch mixed with 3 tablespoons water

Using a high flame, heat a frying pan with ½ tablespoon oil and ½ teaspoon salt and fry pork chops till done. Remove and cut into 1-inch squares, taking out the bones. Heat pan again with 1 tablespoon oil and 1 teaspoon salt. Add tomato, heart of celery, onions, lettuce and stir-fry for 2 minutes. Add water. Cover and cook for 1 minute. Add meat. Cover and cook for 1 minute. Add catsup, Worcestershire sauce, sugar, monosodium glutamate, pepper and cornstarch paste. Cook and stir for ½ minute.

I am always constantly surprised as to how my mother, like other Chinese-American women, discovers American dishes and makes adaptations of them. She gave her bit of philosophy about this to my wife when we were first married: "If not taste right today, cook again tomorrow, not good tomorrow, cook again next week." Her natural inclination toward cooking has won her not only the respect of those in the community but also first prize in an international cooking contest held some years ago in which foods of all nations were entered. Her motto is "Never use a recipe book" (if everyone were like Mom I would not be writing this book). She uses her sense of smell, taste and sight. Since she has never eaten in an Italian restaurant, I often wonder how she is able to make such delicious spaghetti sauce.

SPAGHETTI SAUCE WITH GROUND PORK

1 diced onion	1 can tomato paste
2 cloves crushed garlic	4 tablespoons sugar
1 pound ground pork	¾ teaspoon salt
1 can tomatoes (1 lb. 12 oz.)	

Using a high flame, heat a well-greased frying pan and add 1 clove crushed garlic. Add onion and stir-fry for 5 minutes. Remove and set aside. Heat and grease the pan again and add 1 clove crushed garlic. Add ground pork and stir-fry for 5 minutes. Add tomatoes, tomato paste, 2 tomato-paste cans of water, sugar and salt and cook over medium heat for 45 minutes. Add pork and onions and cook for another 15 minutes.

Many Chinese mothers use spaghetti in place of Chinese egg noodles when they don't have a chance to buy them in Chinatown. It serves as a substitute in making lo mein.

SPAGHETTI LO MEIN

¼ package thin spaghetti	¼ cup water
½ teaspoon salt	1 tablespoon oyster sauce
1 cup shredded Chinese	(or soy sauce)
cabbage (bok choy)	1 teaspoon monosodium
½ cup bean sprouts	glutamate
¼ pound shredded roast	½ teaspoon sugar
pork (char shu)	dash of pepper

Bring 2 quarts of water to a full rolling boil. Add spaghetti. Boil until tender, stirring often. Drain. Into a very hot well-greased frying pan place salt. Add celery cabbage, bean sprouts, roast pork. Stir-fry for 2 minutes. Add water and place spaghetti on top of vegetables. Cover and cook for 2 minutes. Add oyster sauce, monosodium glutamate, sugar and pepper and mix well.

Sometimes the Chinese adapt an American name for a Chinese dish. One time I telephoned my mother to tell her that we were having an unexpected guest for dinner and asked her what we were having for dinner. She answered that we were having stew that night. I was a bit disappointed because I wanted my friend to try some Chinese food but when we got home what my mother called "stew" was something totally Chinese. It consisted of water lily root and stew beef.

STEW CHINESE STYLE

1 pound stew beef	½ pound water lily root
½ of a ginger root	2 tablespoons soy sauce
1 tablespoon oil	2 tablespoons oyster sauce
½ teaspoon salt	1 teaspoon sugar
1 tablespoon sherry	1 teaspoon monosodium
1 quart water	glutamate
2 pieces star anise (bot gok)	dash of pepper

Pound ginger root with back of large knife. Using a high flame, heat a pot with oil, salt and ginger root. Stir-fry beef for 10 minutes, sprinkling sherry over the meat. Add water and all other ingredients and simmer for 1½ hours.

Even hamburgers have not escaped the ingenuity of the Chinese-Americans, who seem determined to prove that there is no American dish which cannot be improved with a bit of Chinese flavoring.

HAMBURGERS

½ pound ground beef
½ cup diced onions
¼ cup diced green peppers
½ teaspoon monosodium glutamate

1½ teaspoons soy sauce
½ teaspoon sugar
dash of pepper
½ teaspoon salt
2 teaspoons cornstarch

Mix, make patties and fry or broil. The purpose of the cornstarch is to make the beef smoother, and hold the juices inside the patty.

I was never able to understand why most American children disliked spinach until I went to college and ate some of that horribly overcooked, green, mushy stuff which someone explained to me was spinach. In Chinese homes spinach is always one of the favorite vegetables because it is so delicious and saladlike. I'm sure that your children will like spinach too if you cook it the way Chinese mothers do.

SPINACH (CHOW BOR CHOY)

1 pound fresh spinach (bor choy)
1 tablespoon oil
½ teaspoon salt or to taste

1 clove crushed garlic
½ teaspoon monosodium glutamate
2 tablespoons butter

Using a high flame, heat a frying pan with oil, salt and garlic. Stir-fry spinach for 2 minutes (chow). Add monosodium glutamate. Cover and cook for 3 minutes. Remove from stove and add butter.

VARIATION:

SPINACH WITH CHINESE CHEESE
(CHOW BOR CHOY FOO YU)

Prepare the same way and add 4 cakes Chinese cheese (foo yu) and ½ teaspoon sugar just before spinach is done.

One of the favorite meals of the Chinese-American home is Thanksgiving dinner. One would assume that this of all meals would be totally American, but don't underestimate the power of a Chinese matron. She has even improved upon the Thanksgiving turkey. On the surface everything looks normal. We usually have baked potatoes, biscuits, peas and carrots, celery and a huge turkey. But the bit of Oriental cooking will not be found on the surface because on this day it is hidden inside the turkey, in the stuffing. Elsewhere I have never tasted turkey stuffing like this and I don't think that it can even be matched. It is merely adapted from an old Chinese dish called *lor mei gai,* which is stuffed chicken with starchy rice and Chinese sausages. The stuffing is so good that one almost forgets about the turkey itself. As a matter of fact my mother, like other Chinese, eats only the stuffing because she does not like turkey.

THANKSGIVING TURKEY CANTONESE

16-pound turkey
3 cups starchy rice (lor mei)
6 cups water
1 cup diced walnuts
½ cup Chinese mushrooms
   (dung goo)
2 tablespoons oil
7½ teaspoons salt
1 cup diced onions

½ pound diced Chinese
   sausage (lop chong)
½ cup diced green peppers
2½ teaspoons monosodium
   glutamate
2 teaspoons soy sauce
½ teaspoon sugar
dash of pepper
1 cup sliced onions

cornstarch to thicken

Wash starchy rice in water by rubbing the grains between palms until water is clear. Cook with six cups of water in same manner as rice (see p. 166). Boil walnuts for ½ hour. Soak mushrooms for ½ hour. Drain and dice. Using a high flame, heat a frying pan with 1 tablespoon oil and 1 tablespoon salt. Add diced onions, sausage and mushrooms. Stir-fry for 1 minute. Add green peppers and stir-fry for 3 minutes. Mix with rice, 3½ teaspoons salt, 1½ teaspoons monosodium glutamate, 1 tablespoon oil, sugar, pepper, walnuts and soy sauce. Stuff the turkey. Place sliced onions on the bottom of a large roasting pan and place turkey on this. (The purpose of this is to prevent burning of the turkey skin.) Pour 3 quarts of water in pan. Bake at 450° F. for 20 minutes. Baste. Bake 10 minutes more. Turn the turkey over. Reduce heat to 350° F. Bake 40 minutes more, turning turkey over every 10 minutes. Remove turkey. Bring gravy to boil and add 1 teaspoon salt and 1 teaspoon monosodium glutamate and enough cornstarch to thicken.

3. Americans in Chinatown

New York's Chinatown in my grandfather's day was colorful and at times dangerous. Most of the men still wore pigtails and the traditional clothing of China. Tong wars, which were the fights between associations seeking control of gambling interests, took place only yards away from our restaurant. All this is hard to believe today in view of the fact that Chinatown has a very low crime rate and little juvenile delinquency. As a matter of fact the only time that you hear about tong wars today is when you listen to a tourist guide's "spiel" in Chinatown. Within these five square blocks is a conservative world of industrious and provident people. All tourists and New Yorkers as well enjoy just walking along Mott Street observing the people on this street, listening to fragments of conversation in singsong Chinese dialects, and stopping now and then to window-shop. The shops are stocked with idols of ivory, rosewood and bronze, jade earrings and necklaces. Occasionally you may see an elderly woman whose slight gait reveals that her feet had been bound when she was a little girl in China. Most of the younger women wear American clothing.

Chinatown is particularly interesting on Sundays because that is the day that Chinese living within a radius of 50 miles come into town for business and pleasure with their whole family. On Sunday these people buy all the Chinese groceries and vegetables which they will need for the rest of the week. They visit relatives, friends and village societies, eat lunch and dinner at a restaurant, see their doctors and dentists, and then perhaps play a friendly game of Mah Jong or go to the Chinese moviehouse which shows films imported from Hong Kong. Sunday is the day that they look forward to because most of these people are laundrymen who have worked conscientiously but lonesomely at their little stores all over the New York and New Jersey area without anyone to talk to or to visit. Sunday is a day of smiling faces and constant chatter until nightfall when each one of them carries his large package of Chinese groceries, neatly and securely tied, back home to his little shop.

Names of restaurants take up much of the space in the canopy of signs over the sidewalks of Chinatown, where almost every building is occupied by one or more places of business. Occasionally one will find other establishments which are not Chinese, for persons of German, Irish and Italian descent are still to be found in this district that has not always been Chinatown. During the seventy-odd years since this section became predominantly Chinese it has in some ways changed less than any other foreign settlement in New York.

Chinatown is especially a wonderful place late at night.

Walking around the streets after midnight one will find that most of the coffee shops and food shops are filled with old men arguing about philosophy. The younger men concern themselves with news of current events and business although you could never get into a conversation with any of them without his referring to the good old days in China when . . .

The story of Chinatown is not just that of its growth, its neon lights and new modern restaurants. The inside story of Chinatown is the change in the philosophy of its people. For three generations the people have tried to keep some of their customs and manners but even this tie to the old world is becoming weak. Perhaps the only time in the year that many of the youngsters really show their Chinese heritage is during New Year when the streets are popping with firecrackers and the dragon dancers appear.

To an American nothing is so exotic as the Chinese grocery store. Walking along Mott Street you can see large displays of Chinese vegetables, spices and meats in the store windows. Walking into one of these grocery stores you will be enchanted by the odor of fresh and dried fish, Chinese sausages and fresh vegetables mingled with the aroma of unfamiliar spices. Here the mystifying components of Chinese meals are displayed side by side with American staples. Among the produce is BOK CHOY, Chinese celery cabbage,

which looks like celery and cabbage crossed. It is one of the
most popular vegetables found in Chinese restaurants in
America. Bok choy is a very leafy green vegetable with white
stems and is excellent for stir-fry dishes as well as for soup.

Melons of all sizes and shapes never cease to fascinate vis-
itors to the Chinese grocery stores. The most conspicuous is
the DUNG QUAR, winter melon. It has the size and shape of a
large pumpkin with a frosty-looking greenish-white skin. The
inside is filled with a white pulp which makes a delicious
soup.

Your attention may be caught by a dark green vegetable
about eight inches long and three inches in diameter with
a hard-looking skin which reminds you of alligator skin. This

unusual-looking vegetable is FOOH QUAR, bitter melon, which is especially popular with the Chinese in the summer because it leaves the mouth with a slightly cool flavor somewhat like mints. Because Americans do not like the taste, it is rarely served in Chinese restaurants.

Alongside these melons one may find Chinese snow pea pods (SOOT DOW) which are used sparingly in many Chinese dishes. They are very difficult to grow and consequently often cost twice as much as steak per pound. In spite of this, soot dow is very popular because it is one of the finest examples of the subtlety of Chinese cooking.

Other green vegetables on display are GUY CHOY, a green leafy vegetable with stronger flavor than bok choy; Chinese broccoli (GUY LON) which looks like its American counterpart but is more tender and subtle in flavor; and hairy melon (JEET QUAR), medium green in color and covered with fine spines.

Quite prominent in any window display of Chinese vegetables is the reddish-brown underwater stem of the water lily called LIEN NGOW. This wonderful root about a yard long is sliced into thin pieces and cooked for several hours with beef and various herbs to make a dark-colored soup. In the same shelf with the lien ngow is usually found a small light brown

root about three inches long, fresh ginger root. Ginger root is almost essential in cooking any stir-fried Chinese dish and is an absolute necessity when cooking fish, because it serves as a deodorizer and adds a tangy flavor to cooking.

Moving away from the vegetable department of the Chinese grocery, you might ask about meat and fowl. On entering the store you were struck by the sight of whole roast ducks hung up by their necks and glistening with a coating of brown soy sauce, several racks of roast pork, and believe it or not a whole roast pig hanging at the meat counter with its crisp brown skin and tender meat. These smoked meats and fowl, served hot or as cold cuts, are among the choicest flavors in Chinese cookery. Moving around the store you will find several large pickle barrels filled with pickled cabbage (SHUEN CHOY) which is very tasty when stir-fried with beef. Another contains salted eggs (HOM DON) soaking in brine. These eggs are simply boiled and eaten with plain rice for a "lazy man's" dinner.

Perhaps the most interesting of the condiments used in authentic Chinese cooking is the lowly soy bean. Some species of the soy have a larger oil content than the peanut, and all known species of the bean have a larger content of oil than have olives. After the oil has been extracted by pressing at low heat, the husks of the bean are removed to form the base of soy sauce, an ingredient which can now be bought at any supermarket. The pulp of the bean is ground to make a curd extremely high in protein content. These bean curds (DOW FOO) look somewhat like little rectangles of white custard and can be boiled, stir-fried or baked. Some of the fresh bean curd is permitted to ferment, making a richly aromatic and tangy cheese. Commonly called Chinese cheese, FOO YU is sold in bottles and does not require any cooking.

The shelves in the grocery will be filled with cans of water chestnuts (MAR TAI) and bamboo shoots (JOOK SOON). Good fresh water chestnuts are very difficult to get so that it is better to buy them in cans. They are sold in most supermarkets. Water chestnuts are valued for some medicinal properties, but claims for their efficacy are vague. They have no taste of their own but they add a wonderful crispness to the food. The bamboo shoots are used in cooking because of their crispness and sweetness.

A very popular sauce which is sold in cans or bottles is sweet and sour sauce, more commonly called duck sauce (SHUEN MOY JEUNG). This sauce, made from apricots and plums, is used for dipping meats such as spare ribs or roast pork and egg rolls. HAISEIN SAUCE, a thick red sauce used as an ingredient in cooking spare ribs, is also sold in cans. Oyster sauce, HO YOW, is a thick brown liquid which is salty in taste and is often used for dipping plain boiled chicken or roast pig. Dow SEE are small fermented beans which are used commonly for seafoods such as strong-smelling fish, shrimps or lobsters. They have a delightful spicy flavor and should be rinsed in water and crushed before using. Also among the canned and bottled sauces you will find MIEN SEE, a spicy, thick, aromatic sauce made from brown beans. It is usually used with steamed fish dishes but it has not been very popular with the American taste probably because of its unusually spicy flavor.

Because of the lack of refrigeration in old China, the Chinese very early learned how to dry foods. Thus in the Chinese grocery you will find large jars of dried scallops (GONG YU CHEE) and dried shrimps (HAR MEI). These have to be soaked before cooking and are usually used for soups. Dried lily flowers, GUM JUM, is literally translated as "golden needles." They are used like a vegetable with fish, poultry and vegetables.

The only thing that we have missed on this guided tour of a Chinese grocery store are some of the unusual spices which are kept out of sight in tiers of little drawers in the back of the store. Some of these spices are dried tangerine peel (gwor pay), cardamom seeds, Chinese cinnamon (jook gwuy), red dates (hong jo), and cloud's ears (wun yee). None of these appear in the recipes because they are so rarely used. When properly cared for (at about the age of 100 years), the shrunken and gnarled peel of a single tangerine is worth about $25 in the retail market in this country. Today, dried tangerine peels are difficult to come by, except those somewhat younger than a century old. "Five-flavored powder" (NG HEUNG FUN) is concocted of powdered cinnamon bark, cardamom and ground ginger. The other ingredients (and they are mixed) remain the manufacturer's secrets. Five-flavored powder may be used in Braised Boneless Duck (Wor Shu Opp) in place of leung leel named in the recipe or in Roast Duck (For Opp) in place of yuen see, far jeel and bok gok. Popularly known as star anise, the BOT GOK (eight horns) is a delight to the Chinese chef. It is a starlike cluster of eight elongated seeds or horns clustered near the lower end to form its starlike appearance. Highly pungent, its habitat is in the lush loam of southern China. It is used in Chinese Mushrooms (Mun Dung Gwo) and in Stew Chinese Style.

GUIDE TO CHINESE INGREDIENTS

INGREDIENT	HOW IT IS SOLD AND WHERE	RECIPES
MEAT		
Pork Sausage Lop Chong	Sold by piece, only in Chinese groceries	Steamed Ground Pork with Chinese Pork Sausage (Lop Chong Yok Beng) Thanksgiving Turkey Cantonese
Roast Chicken Shew Gai	Sold whole, only in Chinese groceries	Served hot or cold, not in any recipes
Roast Duck For Opp	Sold whole, only in Chinese groceries	Served hot or cold Roast Duck Lo Mein (For Opp Lo Mein)
Roast Pig For Yook	Sold by pound, only in Chinese groceries	Served hot or cold, not in any recipes
Roast Pork Char Shu	Sold by pound, only in Chinese groceries	Served cold, or in any roast pork recipes
FISH		
Dried Scallops Gong Yu Chee	Sold by ounce. Soak 45 minutes in cold water before using	Congee (Jook) optional Hairy Melon Soup (Jee Quar Tong)
Dried Shrimp Har Mei	Sold by ounce. Wash and soak for 20 minutes	Congee (Jook) optional Cellophane Noodles with Pork (Fun See Gee Yok)

INGREDIENT	HOW IT IS SOLD AND WHERE	RECIPES
	VEGETABLES	
Bamboo Shoots Jook Soon	Canned. Available in supermarkets. After can is opened, keep in water in refrigerator and change water every other day. Used for taste and texture	In many recipes
Bean Sprouts Ngar Choy	Sold fresh by pound. Also sold in supermarkets canned. Spoil easily. Used for taste, texture and as stretcher	In many recipes
Bitter Melon Fooh Quar	Sold by pound. Remove spongy pulp and seeds before cooking. Has cool and slightly bitter flavor	Bitter Melon with Beef (Fooh Quar Ngow) Bitter Melon with Pork (Fooh Quar Gee)
* Black Beans Dow See	Sold by ounce. Wash and soak for 10 minutes before using	Lobster Cantonese (Chow Lung Har) Beef with Green Peppers and Tomatoes (Fon Care Lot Tzu Ngow) Pork with Tomatoes (Fon Care Gee)
Chinese Broccoli Guy Lon	Sold fresh by pound. American broccoli may be substituted	Pork with Broccoli (Guy Lon Gee Yok) Beef with Broccoli (Guy Lon Ngow)

INGREDIENT	HOW IT IS SOLD AND WHERE	RECIPES
Chinese Celery Cabbage Bok Choy	Sold fresh by pound at Chinese or Japanese groceries. Used for taste, texture and as stretcher. Celery or celery cabbage may be substituted	In many recipes
Chinese Green Cabbage Guy Choy	Green leafy vegetable with stronger flavor than bok choy	Beef with Chinese Green Cabbage (Guy Choy Ngow)
Chinese Mushrooms Dung Goo	Dried. Sold by ounce. Soak in cold water for ½ hour before using. Dried mushrooms sold in supermarkets may be substituted	In many recipes
Chinese Parsley Yuen Sai	Sold by pound in Chinese groceries. Has a distinctive taste different from American parsley	Duck with Parsley (Sy Wu Opp)
Chinese White Mushrooms Seen Gwoo	Sold by ounce in Chinese groceries	Winter Melon Soup (Dung Quar Jung)
Hairy Melon Jeet Quar	Sold in Chinese groceries	Hairy Melon Soup (Jeet Quar Tong)
Pickled Cabbage Shuen Choy	Sold in bulk. Used for stir-fry dishes	Beef with Pickled Cabbage (Shuen Choy Ngow)

INGREDIENT	HOW IT IS SOLD AND WHERE	RECIPES
Salted Cabbage Chung Choy	Dried. Sold by ounce. Wash and soak for 15 minutes in cold water before using. Used for soups and steamed dishes	Steamed Pork with Salted Cabbage (Chung Choy Jing Gee Yok)
Snow Peas Soot Dow	Sold fresh by pound at Chinese groceries. Best in fall and early winter. Used for texture and very subtle taste	In many recipes
Winter Melon Dung Quar	Sold by pound at Chinese groceries. Used mainly for soup	Winter Melon Soup (Dung Quar Tong)

SEASONINGS AND SAUCES

* Bean Curds Dow Foo	Sold fresh or canned in Chinese or Japanese groceries	Beef with Bean Curds (Dow Foo Ngow) Steamed Fish with Bean Curds (Dow Foo Jing Yu) Bean Curd Soup (Dow Foo Tong)
* Brown Bean Sauce Mien See	Sold canned in Chinese groceries	Beef with String Beans (Dow Jai Ngow) Steamed Fish (Jing Yu) Steamed Fish with Bean Curds (Dow Foo Jing Yu) Duck with Potatoes (Shee Jai Opp)

INGREDIENT	HOW IT IS SOLD AND WHERE	RECIPES
Duck Sauce Shuen Moy Jeung	Sold bottled or canned in Chinese groceries. Used as condiment	Roast Pork (Char Shu) Egg Rolls (Chuen Guen)
Far Jeel	A dried spice sold by the ounce in Chinese groceries or drugstores	Roast Duck (For Opp)
* Ginger Root Sang Gueng	Sold by ounce at Chinese groceries. Will keep for several months. Omit from recipe if it can't be bought fresh. Very important as deodorizer in preparing fish	In many recipes
Golden Needles Gum Jum	Dried lily flowers. Soak in cold water for 15 minutes before using	Fried Fish with Chinese Vegetables (Hung Shew Yu) optional Chinese Celery Cabbage (Chow Bok Choy) optional Chicken in Chinese Mushroom Sauce (Dung Goo Wat Gai) optional
Haisein Sauce	Sold canned or bottled in Chinese groceries. Used chiefly as condiment	Barbecue Spare Ribs (Shew Pai Quot) Meat Patties (Shu Mei)
Leung Leel	A dried spice sold by the ounce in Chinese groceries and drugstores	Braised Boneless Duck (Wor Shew Opp)

INGREDIENT	HOW IT IS SOLD AND WHERE	RECIPES
Lotus Seed Lien Jee	Sold by ounce in Chinese groceries	Winter Melon Soup (Dung Quar Jung)
Monosodium Glutamate Mei Jing	Used to enhance taste. No flavor of its own. Sold at supermarkets under various names	In many recipes
Nom Yee	A dried spice sold by the ounce in Chinese groceries and drugstores	Duck with Potatoes (Shee Jai Opp)
One Hundred Unities Baak Haap	Dried spice seldom used in ordinary cooking. Sold in Chinese groceries	Winter Melon Soup (Dung Quar Jung)
* Oyster Sauce Ho Yow	Bottled. Sold in Chinese groceries. Used for condiment and cooking. Is *not* interchangeable with soy sauce	Pork with Oyster Sauce (Ho Yow Gee Yok) Squab with Oyster Sauce (Ho Yow Bok Opp) Spaghetti Lo Mein Beef with Oyster Sauce (Ho Yow Ngow) Beef with Bean Curd (Dow Foo Ngow) Roast Pork with Bean Curd (Dow Foo Char Shu) Chicken Wings with Oyster Sauce (Ho Yow Gai Yick)
Soy Sauce See Yow	Bottled and canned. Sold in Chinese groceries and American supermarkets. Avoid heavy bitter concentrates	In many recipes

INGREDIENT	HOW IT IS SOLD AND WHERE	RECIPES
Star Anise Bok Gok	Eight elongated seeds in a starlike cluster. It is highly pungent. Not used often	Chinese Mushrooms (Mun Dung Goo) Stew Chinese Style
Water Lily Root Lien Ngow	Sold by ounce. Reddish-brown underwater stem of water lily	Stew Chinese Style
Yuen See	A dried spice sold by the ounce in Chinese groceries and drugstores	Roast Duck (For Opp)

OTHER

Bird's Nest	Sold in boxes	Bird's Nest Soup (Gai Yung Yeen Wor)
Cellophane Noodles Fun See	Sold in boxes. Wash and soak for 10 minutes before using. Vermicelli may be substituted	Beef with Cellophane Noodles (Fun See Ngow) Pork with Cellophane Noodles (Fun See Gee Yok)
Chinese Cheese Foo Yu	Sold in bottles in Chinese groceries	Spinach Cantonese with Chinese Cheese (Chow Bor Choy)
Egg Noodles Don Mein	Sold fresh and dried by pound in Chinese and Japanese groceries. Also in supermarkets	Roast Pork Lo Mein (Char Shu Lo Mein)
Egg Roll Wrappers	Sold in Chinese groceries. Keep in refrigerator. Will become hard and dry if not used within a week	Egg Rolls (Chuen Guen)

	HOW IT IS SOLD AND	
INGREDIENT	WHERE	RECIPES
Fried Noodles Jow Mein	Sold by pound in Chinese groceries and at supermarkets	Chicken Chow Mein Subgum Chow Mein
Salted Eggs Hom Don	Eaten boiled or steamed with pork	Steamed Ground Pork with Salted Egg (Hom Don Jing Gee Yok)
Starchy Rice Lor Mei	Sold by pound in Chinese groceries	Thanksgiving Turkey
Wonton	Sold by pound in Chinese groceries	Meat Patties (Shu Mei) Fried Wonton Wonton Soup

* The starred items, which have no substitutes, are highly desired for many recipes and available only in Chinese groceries or by mail from the following companies. The other, less often used ingredients may also be ordered from these companies.

California:
  Yee Sing Chong Company
  950 Castelar Street
  Los Angeles, Calif.
  Shew Hing Lung Company
  832 Grant Avenue
  San Francisco, Calif.

Illinois:
  Mee Jun Mercantile
    Company
  2223 Wentworth Ave.
  Chicago 16, Ill.
  Sun Wah Hing
    Trading Company
  2246 Wentworth Avenue
  Chicago, Ill.

Massachusetts:
  Tai Kwong Company
  60 Beach Street
  Boston, Mass.

Michigan:
  Lun Yick Company
  1339 Third Avenue
  Detroit, Mich.

New York:
  Mon Fong Wo Company
  36 Pell Street
  New York, N. Y.
  Wing Fat Company
  35 Mott Street
  New York, N. Y.

Ohio:
  Sun Lee Yuen Company
  1726 Payne Avenue
  Cleveland, Ohio

Pennsylvania:
  Yick Fung Company
  210 North Ninth Street
  Philadelphia, Pennsylvania

4. Bringing China into Your Home

A bit of China has been brought into many American homes through the means of decorations such as Chinese vases, rugs, tapestries, brass bowls, porcelains, and teakwood furniture. The fun and pleasure of having Chinese things, however, has not been confined to the living room but has spread to the kitchen of many homes. Carefully placed next to the silver setting one can sometimes find a set of ivory chopsticks or fine porcelain soup spoons. Chinese porcelain rice bowls, purchased primarily for serving Chinese meals, are often used for serving soup and exotic dessert dishes.

1. UTENSILS

Those who have gone all out have among their prized possessions in the kitchen a *wock* (a rounded-bottom circular pan), a *choy doh* (a knife for both meats and vegetables) and perhaps even a picture of the kitchen god, Joh Quon.

It does not matter whether you have all these Chinese

things in your kitchen because there probably is not an American kitchen which does not have the utensils needed for Chinese cooking or which can at least be adapted for Chinese cooking. All that is needed, basically, is a good supply of lidded pots and pans, a steamer, a good stove, and good organization and co-ordination on the part of the chef.

If you have ever peeked into the kitchen of a Chinese restaurant you would have seen several *wocks*. The Chinese *wock* is hammered out of iron or copper with a diameter of 12 inches in the family size. These pans are the best for Chinese cooking because heat is concentrated on the center of the pan for quick stir-frying. The flared sides of the pan permit the cook to use less oil. Very often a chef is judged by whether his food has *wock hay*, the flavor of the *wock*. To have *wock hay* the food after it is cooked must be crisp in texture, the vegetables must look as fresh as before they were cooked, smell delicious, and yet not be burnt. A *wock* can also be used as a deep-fat fryer. An attractive addition to any kitchen, it may be purchased in a grocery or hardware store in any Chinatown. It is not of course an absolute necessity. As a matter of fact we have been using a large deep frying pan at home instead of the *wock* for many years. It is important that your frying pan is large and deep enough for stir-frying so that you can stir the food without ending up with half of the food on the floor or on the stove.

The *jing loong* is used for steaming. Its principle is a double boiler with a perforated bottom. You can use a large pot and put a rack on the bottom and add water in the pan up to the rack. Then you place the dish containing the ingredients which you are steaming on top of the rack and cover the pot. After the water is boiling, turn the heat low. Add some more water later if the water is evaporating.

For cutting, the Chinese chef uses a *choy doh,* the cutting knife for both vegetables and meat. Although American kitchen knives will serve the purpose they are not as versatile. Our chefs use the *choy doh* for every kind of cutting in the kitchen, which includes coarse and fine dicing of vegetables and meats, slicing of meats and vegetables, boning and chopping of chickens and ducks, boning fish, chopping lobsters, and mincing meats. The broad blade is used to carry foods from the chopping block to the *wock*. Incidentally, Americans will find that partially freezing meats makes it easier to slice them evenly.

One of the first things that a Chinese chef learns is how to use the *choy doh*. It is probably the most important thing in the art of Chinese cooking. With it, the dishes will look good, uniform and appetizing. No matter how delicious your gravy is, a dish of food will not be pleasing to the eye and thus psychologically pleasing to the palate if the vegetables and meats have been sloppily or carelessly cut. Uneven slicing also leads to uneven cooking of the food. Most important, because there has always been a shortage of food in China, a good chef with a knife will not waste a scrap of food because he knows where to cut and how to cut it.

The *jum bahn,* chopping block, is used in all Chinese restaurants. It is usually 18 inches in diameter and about 6 inches in height and comes from a tree trunk. For your home, any good chopping board will do just as well.

Other accessories and light cooking utensils are not much different from the ordinary ladle, pancake turner, and draining spoon which are found in the American home, although the Chinese often use chopsticks for taking things out of hot pans.

2. Preparation

The cooking of Chinese food requires a maximum of preparation and a minimum of cooking. You cannot over-emphasize the importance of careful slicing or cutting meats and vegetables and the careful organization of ingredients and spices so that you know where everything is *before* you start cooking. Most of the dishes in this book will take no

more than 6 minutes of cooking time, consequently you will
have to be very well organized so that nothing is overcooked
or burned.

a. *Methods of cutting*

There are various methods of cutting Chinese food. You
will also find that if the meats for a particular dish are to
be sliced into long strips, then the vegetables will also be
of the same shape. If you are making diced chicken with
vegetables and almonds (Gai ding), in which the chicken is
diced, then you may be sure that the large vegetables too
have to be diced. The obvious reason for this is that it will
make the dish look much better and neater, but besides this
there is a practical reason. Cutting the different ingredients
into the same shape makes a uniformity in its texture and
its taste. Also, with chopsticks it is very difficult to pick up
different sizes, such as a piece of diced meat with a long thin
piece of vegetable.

(1) Slicing (Peen)

Straight slicing is used for meats and vegetables such as
mushrooms, scallions and other fleshy and fibrous vegetables.

Meat is cut against the grain, i.e. at right angles to the direction of the fibers, and into pieces ⅛-inch thick.

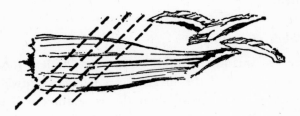

Diagonal slicing is used for slicing vegetables such as Chinese celery cabbage (bok choy) and other stalklike vegetables so that there will be a larger area exposed to the heat in cooking and in absorbing flavors.

(2) Dicing (Ding)

The meat or vegetable is cut into little cubes varying from ½ to ⅛th of an inch depending on the dish.

(3) Chopping (Soong)

There will be some dishes which will require fine chopping. Sometimes the meat grinder will not do a fine enough job of it. The Chinese chef will use a Chinese vegetable knife and chop until the pieces become fine (1/16 inch).

(4) Chunk (Kow)

Cut in chunks about 1 inch square, as in Sweet and Sour Pork (Niu Yok) or Fried Shrimp With Vegetables (Chow Har Kow)

(5) Shredding (Sze)

Cut in 1½ inch long by ⅛ inch strips, as in Roast Pork (Char Shu)

b. *Organization*

Since Chinese cooking is usually "quick cooking" one of the most important things is to have good organization. A difference in one or two minutes in cooking time may mean that your food will come out overcooked, soft, soggy, and tasteless. You will realize how fast the seconds tick away as you have your frying pan cooking something while you suddenly find out that one of your ingredients has not been cut yet or as you try to find the bottle opener for the soy sauce, or as you reach for the dishes you need.

After you have finished preparing the meat and vegetables, you place in one dish each group of ingredients to be added to the cooking together at the same time. It is important to place all your ingredients such as garlic, ginger root, salt, pepper, oil, sugar and cornstarch in an orderly arrangement on a table next to the stove so that you will be able to reach for them when you need them.

3. METHODS OF COOKING

For the beginner, it might be best to cook only one Chinese dish, preparing it with an American meal. Then you might cook another Chinese dish the next time, and so add to your "repertory" until you can cook a whole Chinese meal at once on several burners, knowing then how to time the cooking.

You will probably soon learn the Chinese names for the following methods of cooking, because these words appear in the names of many of the dishes in this book as well as on the menus of Chinese restaurants.

a. *Chow (stir-frying)*

This is the most popular method of Chinese cooking and is called either stir-frying or sautéing at high heat. Most food in Chinese restaurants is prepared in this manner. Its principle is a very hot pan, very little oil (about 1 tablespoon), and no more than 6 minutes of cooking time. The quick cooking preserves the flavor, texture and coloring of the food, especially vegetables, and so little oil is used that the calorie content is lower than in dishes cooked in the Western fashion.

A lightly greased frying pan is heated very hot, then the vegetables are tossed in and stirred. A little water is added and then the pan is covered. (See the recipes for the precise timing and procedure.) American vegetables such as spinach and broccoli prepared by this method are far more delightful than when prepared by the boiled method.

b. *Shew (roasting)*

Meats such as spare ribs and pork are roasted on a rack or spit over direct heat and basted with a seasoned sauce. An ordinary home oven can be used.

c. *Jow (deep frying)*

This is the same as the American way of deep frying. The food is fried to a golden brown outside and is cooked on the inside, as in Duck With Parsley (Sy Wu Opp).

d. *Jing (steaming)*

The ingredients are cooked with wet steam. Refer back to the discussion on the steamer *(jing lung)* on page 59 to see how you would do steaming at home. This method of cooking is important to learn because this dish can be cooking by itself on one range while you are stir-frying something else.

e. *Mun (fricasseeing)*

The food is first braised and then simmered in stock or sauce until cooked. The effect of this is to smother the food with the flavor of the rich sauce and yet keep the vegetables and meats crisp.

f. *Hoong shew (red-roasting)*

The ingredients are first braised and then put into a double boiler with plenty of soup stock. This method of cooking is generally used for preparation of things prepared with herbs and not everyday dishes.

4. TIMING

Chinese food has to be eaten while it is hot. One of the problems which most housewives (including Chinese housewives) have is how to prepare a meal so that everything will be hot when it is placed on the table. You will find that cooking something and attempting to keep it hot for more than 5 minutes by covering it will usually tend to ruin your cooking because the steam from the hot dish of food will soften all of the vegetables in it.

If you are planning a complete Chinese meal for a family of four and you have a stove with four burners, what will you do? One burner will be used for the rice and the second will be used for the soup. These items will not have to be watched after they are started. For four people you can either have two main dishes, or even three if you feel ambitious. In order to time your meal so that everything is hot, do not try to attempt more than two stir-fried dishes at one meal. It usually takes 6 minutes to cook a stir-fried dish, and by the time that you are cooking the third dish fifteen minutes will have gone by and the first dish will be cold and soggy. Instead of doing that you should plan to have a steamed dish which would not require your constant attention. In this way all of the food will be ready at the same time.

It is very important that a beginner learn how to prepare Chinese food in an orderly fashion and I would suggest that you do things in the following order:

1. Wash rice and measure the amount of water that is needed and put on top of the stove until you are ready to start cooking it. Approximate cooking time is twenty minutes, so you can turn on the flame 20 minutes before you plan to eat.
2. Prepare the ingredients for your steamed dish or roasted dish and place on stove ready to cook at any time, timing it precisely for the time you want to serve it.
3. Prepare the ingredients for your stir-fried dishes. This usually involves a lot of cutting and slicing which may take a beginner from half an hour to an hour until he is more sure of himself.

Be sure to place all your ingredients including the right amount of salt, pepper, sugar, seasoning powder, soy sauce, and cornstarch paste within reach so that you will not have to hunt for them later or try to measure the right amounts while everything is burning.

5. Serving Chinese

The names of Chinese dishes always confuse and mystify Americans. Actually most of these names can be learned very easily because they are made up of words that describe the ingredient, the manner of preparation, and the method of cooking.

In Chapter 1 with the help of the seasoning chart you find the Chinese names for ingredients. In Chapter 4 you find the words describing the way the meat and vegetables in the dish are prepared: peen or pan (slicing); ding (dicing); soong (chopping); kow (chunks); and sze (shredding). Finally you find at the end of Chapter 4 the terms for the various methods of Chinese cooking: chow (stir-frying); shew (roasting); jow (deep frying); jing (steaming); mun (fricasseeing); and hoong shew (red-roasting). Now with these terms you will be able to identify more than half of a Chinese menu.

Let us take the dish Chow har kow and try to figure out what it is. As a general rule the first word tells the method of cooking which is used in making the dish. In this case we know that *chow* means stir-frying and thus we know that this is a stir-fry dish. The word or words in the middle usually tell us the main ingredient or ingredients. The word *har* means shrimp.

The last word in the name of the dish very often tells us the manner in which the ingredients were cut or sliced. Thus we know that Chow har *kow* has ingredients which are cut into chunks.

Therefore we can know that Chow har kow is a stir-fried dish with chunks of shrimp. We can assume that it will be served with vegetables because most Chinese stir-fried dishes have vegetables in them.

Very often the first adjective is left out, in which case we can assume that it is a stir-fried dish because that is the most popular in Cantonese cooking. Gai ding is diced chicken with vegetables, stir-fried.

Sometimes the name has no adjectives at all but only the names of the ingredients. In this case it is fair to assume that it is a stir-fried dish in which the meat and vegetables are sliced. An example is Bok choy ngow yook, which is Chinese cabbage with beef. There are, of course, many exceptions to the rule but at least you have a key to the names of dishes and can order with some familiarity the next time you go to a Chinese restaurant.

1. How to order in a Chinese restaurant

The Chinese way of eating is quite different from the American way. At American dinners, each person orders something for himself and he eats only that particular dish. The Chinese, on the other hand, place all the dishes at the center of the table and everyone shares in them. There is no main course such as a roast, of which everyone has an individual portion. Instead, all the courses are put on the table at the same time and shared by all. At home, you might have three main dishes and rice for four or more people.

When ordering in a Chinese restaurant you should order about one dish for every person present although no general rules can be made here because of the varying size of the dishes. If you have four people you can order a soup, a seafood dish, beef with your favorite vegetables, pork, and perhaps a chicken or egg dish. The idea is to get a well-rounded meal both nutritionwise and in taste and variety.

If you order a sharp-tasting dish like sweet and sour pork, be sure to order something more bland like vegetables to go with it. If you order a dice-cut dish like Char shu ding (dice-cut roast pork with Chinese vegetables) don't order something like Gai ding (dice-cut chicken with Chinese vegetables) which is very similar. Instead you should have something like Moo goo gai peen (sliced chicken with mushrooms and vegetables) which will look different and taste different too.

Too many people are afraid to try new things and a Chinese waiter will normally not try to urge anybody to try something exotic. In fact you will have to assure the waiter that you are adventurous before he will agree to bring you something unusual. The best way to try out new things if you are a bit cautious is to order two or three dishes which you are sure to like and then order one new dish. In this way you will be able to try something new each time you go to a Chinese restaurant and may learn the dishes before you try them at home.

There is only one well-known dish—shark's fin soup—for which I have not given a recipe in this book. Only a few Chinese chefs are able to prepare this properly so that the shark's fin will not melt. To attempt this your kitchen would probably result in a mess. Chinese never attempt its preparation at home.

2. SERVING A CHINESE-AMERICAN DINNER WITH ONE MAIN DISH

Once you have become acquainted with the technique of Chinese cooking you will find that it will take as short a time to prepare a Chinese dinner as it does to prepare an American dinner. In the beginning you will probably want to cook only one main course not only because your family is used to this American form of serving food but also so that you can concentrate on cooking this one dish.

Chinese food can be easily integrated into an American meal and as a matter of fact we do it at home quite often. If you decide to make the Chinese dish the meat dish then all you have to do is to prepare a salad or vegetable with the meal as you would with any American meal. For instance, if you decide to prepare barbecue spare ribs, or roast pork, or lobster Cantonese which has no vegetables in it, then you can prepare a tossed salad, or a frozen vegetable such as peas or broccoli on the side. On the other hand you may decide to prepare an American meat dish and make a Chinese vegetable dish. Perhaps you may decide to make some fried rice to take the place of your normal starch dish of potatoes. There is no right or wrong way to serve a Chinese-American meal at home. Whatever your family enjoys will be the right way. You will find that integrating Chinese cooking with

American cooking will add variety to your meals even if the one Chinese dish happens to be just the soup or a vegetable. Here are a few suggestions. I am sure that you can think of many more.

1. Serve a Chinese soup with an entirely American meal.
2. A Chinese meat dish such as lobster Cantonese, roast pork, or spare ribs with tossed salad and American vegetables.
3. An American meat dish such as steak, chops or chicken with stir-fried spinach or broccoli.
4. An American meat dish such as steak, chops or chicken with a Chinese vegetable dish such as Chinese celery cabbage (bok choy) or bean sprouts.
5. Substitute rice or fried rice or noodles for potatoes.
6. A Chinese dish and your weekend leftovers.

IMPORTANT NOTE: If you are serving a Chinese meat or poultry dish as the main dish of an American meal, it is best to double the amount of meat or poultry in the recipe. Americans are used to more meat than the Chinese, and will not have the several meat dishes that are found in Chinese meals.

There is also another possible variation of the Chinese recipes in this book. Some Americans may prefer a more intensified flavor, and might therefore substitute chicken stock in place of water in the soups, poultry, fish, pork and vegetable recipes. If this is done, the monosodium glutamate may be dropped from the recipe. Those who do this may not develop a taste for some of the more delicate flavors, however, such as that in egg drop soup.

3. EATING CHINESE FAMILY STYLE

After you have tried serving one Chinese dish with your meals, you may want to try cooking a complete Chinese dinner. Once you have learned the technique of Chinese cooking you will find that this will take no more time to cook than an average American meal. You might serve three dishes and rice for four or more people.

4. SUGGESTED MENUS

The following menus are designed to help you plan well-organized and well-balanced meals. Each family will find that it likes certain dishes more than others and soon you will be working out your own menus.

SUGGESTED MENUS FOR FAMILIES OF FOUR

1. Wonton Soup (Wonton Tong)
   Chicken With Mushrooms (Moo Goo Gai Peen)
   Steamed Ground Pork With Ham (For Tui Sing Gee Yok Beng)
   Boiled Rice
2. Egg Drop Soup (Don Far Tong)
   Subgum Egg Foo Young
   Beef With Broccoli (Guy Lon Ngow)
   Breaded Shrimp (Jow Har)
   Boiled Rice
3. Bean Curd Soup (Dow Foo Tong)
   Beef With Green Peppers and Onions (Fon Care Lot Tzu Ngow)
   Roast Pork With Chinese Celery Cabbage (Bok Choy Char Shu)
   Boiled Rice
4. One Chicken Three Flavors (Yat Gai Sam May)
   Yang Chow Fried Rice (Yang Chow Chow Fon)
5. Corn Soup (Gai Yung Sook Mei)
   Roast Duck (For Opp)
   Beef With Chinese Cabbage (Bok Choy Ngow)
   Cantonese Egg Foo Young
6. Minced Chicken With Lettuce Soup (Gai Yung Sang Choy Tong)

Lobster Cantonese (Chow Lung Har)
Subgum Fried Rice (Subgum Chow Fon)
Pork With Beansprouts (Ngar Choy Gee Yok)
7. Water Cress Soup (Sy Yang Choy Tong)
Sweet and Sour Pork Cubes (Niw Goo Yok)
Steamed Eggs (Jing Don)
Diced Chicken With Vegetables (Gai Ding)
Boiled Rice
8. Hairy Melon Soup (Jeet Quar Tong)
Beef With Mushrooms (Moo Goo Ngow)
Butterfly Shrimp (Wor Teap Har)
Diced Pork With Chinese Vegetables (Char Shu Ding)
9. Winter Melon Soup (Dung Quar Jung)
Fried Shrimp With Chinese Vegetables (Chow Har Kow)
Diced Chicken With Walnuts (Hop To Gai Ding)
Beef With Bean Curds (Dow Foo Ngar)
Boiled Rice

5. TABLE SETTING

A Chinese table setting usually consists of a pair of chopsticks, a bowl for soup and rice, a saucer for soy sauce, a porcelain spoon, and a tiny teacup. Soup is usually served first
and then the empty soup bowls are filled with rice. Serving
spoons are never used in the traditional Chinese table setting.
All the dishes are placed on the center of the table where
everyone can reach them. The Chinese prefer round tables
because it makes it easier for each one to reach for everything
on the table. If you are using a long table it may be necessary to divide your portions in half and put them on both
ends of the table so that they can be easily reached. This is
essential because dishes are never passed around the table as
in the American custom.

As far as etiquette is concerned you are supposed to eat
only those pieces which are facing you and you do not reach

for anything which you already have in your bowl until you have finished it. When eating rice it is proper and necessary to hold the bowl up to your mouth with your left hand while you shovel the rice in with the chopsticks on your right hand. The Americans are not used to this and consequently try to pick up grains of rice from their bowl with their chopsticks and by the time it gets to their mouths half of the rice has fallen on the table.

HOW TO HOLD CHOPSTICKS

In holding chopsticks it is very important to know the different function between the upper and the lower chopsticks. The lower chopstick is the stationary one and is held at the base between the thumb and the index finger (A) and the first knuckle of the ring finger (B). The upper chopstick acts as a fulcrum (C). The tips of the index finger and middle finger hold the chopstick farther down on the other end (D). Be sure that the chopsticks are even so that the two ends will meet. When picking up a piece of food the middle finger pushes upward at D so that the tips of the chopsticks are opened in order to fit a piece of food between the tips. Then the index finger pushes down at D so that the tip of the upper chopstick pinches the food against the fixed chopstick.

6. CHINESE BANQUETS

Chinese banquets last over three hours and the number of dishes which are brought out seem endless. The art of eating at a Chinese banquet is to eat no more than a few bites of each dish, otherwise you will never be able to have room to finish the dinner. As contrasted to the informal dinners where everything is brought out at one time, the banquet is served one or two dishes at a time. There is time between each course to drink and talk to your friends. An example of one of these banquets is the one which was held at Lee's Restaurant during its 60th Anniversary.

Appetizers

Har Peen (crisp shrimp chips)
Chiang Gwor (sliced oranges)
Niw Goo Yok (sweet and pungent pork cubes,
     stir-fried in pineapple sauce)

Soup

Dung Quar Yung (chicken broth base with the mashed rind of Chinese winter melon, water lily seeds, sliced imported bamboo shoots, diced chicken, Chinese smoked ham and lobster flakes). The melon, distantly related to both the gourd and the squash, is sometimes steamed and served as the soup bowl itself, with the top cut off for the lid. See page 91 for home-cooked version.

Entrees

Lung Har Guen (lobster rolls, deep-fried, encased in crisp egg noodle batter)

Sy Wu Opp (prepared in a variety of styles, depending upon the whim and skill of the chef. Long Island duckling roasted, then steamed in Chinese parsley, and seasoned with spiced orange rind sauce)

Nor Mei Gai (whole roasted chicken with the bones removed. Stuffed with rice, Chinese spiced ham and spiced sausage, and black imported, spiced Chinese mushrooms)

Tung Gee You Bok Opp (whole roasted squab browned in imported Chinese soy bean sauce. Served dry and crisp)

Fun See Ngow (tenderloin of beef stir-fried with Chinese rich flour noodles, snow pea pods, and water chestnuts). See p. 140 for home-cooked version.

Hung Shew Gai Peen (sliced spring chicken with Chinese ham and selected Chinese vegetables)

Dessert

Traditional Chinese pastry ensemble, symbolizing a wish for longevity, good health, happiness and wealth. (Steamed rice flour buns with red coloring, the good luck color; shrimp dumplings wrapped with a translucent rice flour covering; and Chinese steamed sponge cakes.)

Tea

Flavored with dried aromatic chrysanthemum petals

Most Chinese persons have at least three if not more banquets held in their honor during their lives. The first is called *moon yuet* which is held one month after the baby is born

and is the baby's first birthday party. Red-colored eggs are
served to the guests at the end of the meal symbolizing good
luck and fertility. A second banquet may be held at his wedding. As contrasted to the American custom of the girl's family paying for the wedding and reception, the Chinese allow
each side of the family to throw the banquet. Thus there
may be a banquet given by each family. Very often in Chinatown the crowd overflows one restaurant and thus two or
three restaurants may be used simultaneously for the same
party, and the hosts have to run from one restaurant to the
next to greet their guests. The last banquet in a person's life
is held immediately following the funeral for the people who
go to pay their last respects. This is the only type of banquet
at which fresh fish is served. In China the meal is eaten on
the floor and traditionally bean curd is served to the guests.

150

Chinese Recipes
for
American Kitchens

Appetizers, Pastries, and Desserts

Some Chinese pastries are served at banquets either as appetizers or as desserts, so it is best to describe all three in the same chapter. But the Chinese family dinner at home is complete in itself and is served all at once, including the soup, and there are no appetizers or desserts.

APPETIZERS

Appetizers are served at banquets as a "warm up" for the remaining 14 or 15 courses. Sliced oranges (Chiang gwor) or orange sections are often served at the beginning of a banquet or formal meal and are eaten throughout the meal as a "freshener" between courses. The following appetizers may be found in the recipe section of this book (see Index): fried shrimps (Jow har), fried chicken livers and gizzards (Jow gai gone), fried wonton, deep-fried spare ribs with gravy (So jar pai quot). These are especially well suited for cocktail parties or tea parties, though the Chinese do not have cocktail parties.

A favorite appetizer is of course egg roll (Chuen guen).

EGG ROLL (CHUEN GUEN)

6 tablespoons shredded bamboo shoots	8 cooked shrimp
	½ teaspoon sugar
3 tablespoons shredded water chestnuts	½ teaspoon monosodium glutamate
3 tablespoons shredded celery	dash of pepper
6 tablespoons shredded roast pork (char shu)	½ teaspoon salt
	4 pieces egg roll skin
1 beaten egg	

Using a high flame, heat a well-greased frying pan and add salt. Add all ingredients except egg roll skin and beaten egg. Stir-fry for 3 minutes. Allow to cool. Following the diagram

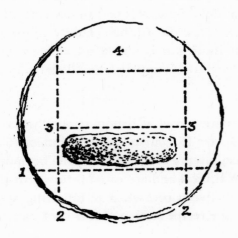

on p. 82, place the mixture on the center of the egg roll skin and fold over two sides. Roll and seal the end with beaten egg. Deep-fry until a rich brown color.

NOTE: Served with duck sauce (see Guide to Chinese Ingredients).

Other dishes which may also be used as American appetizers or cocktail hors d'oeuvres are: butterfly shrimp (Wor teap har), shrimp with tomato sauce (Care jup har), batter-fried shrimp (Jow har), barbecue spare ribs (Shew pai quot), sweet and sour pork cubes (Niw goo yok), sweet and sour spare ribs (Tiem shuen pei quot).

PASTRIES

The meat patties (Shu mei) in this section constitute only one of the assortment of Chinese pastries (dim sum) that are served in teahouses in China. The literal translation of dim sum is "dot heart." Chinese restaurants in the largest American cities will serve these pastries every luncheon or afternoon. In the smaller towns, the Chinese restaurants prepare them only for Sunday afternoon when Chinese customers have come for Sunday shopping. Chinese restaurants in America may serve them with other Chinese dishes, but only on request. They may be ordered to take out.

I have not given the recipes for any of these pastries other than the meat patties for the simple reason that, like shark's fin soup, they cannot be prepared at home either by Chinese or Americans. The delicate transparent covering or skin of these pastries is made of rice flour in a fashion as complicated and involved as the famous French puff paste. Any restaurant that serves the pastries must maintain two staffs, one for the preparation of pastries and the other for the other Chinese dishes.

My father returned to China at one time to learn there how to prepare dim sum, and for a long time our restaurant was the only one in America that served them. The rice flour (gee mei fun) for the translucent covering must be prepared, then filled with meat or shrimp, and steamed. Many Americans find that they must develop a taste for the pastries because, though cooked, the American often mistakenly believes that the covering is uncooked dough merely because of its uncooked appearance.

Shrimp dumpling (Har gow) is filled with shrimp, bamboo shoots and Chinese vegetables. They were served at the 60th Anniversary Banquet of the Lee Restaurant as a dessert (see p. 76).

Minced meat patty (Fun quor) is half-moon shaped, filled with pork, Chinese mushrooms, bamboo shoots, water chestnuts, and Chinese vegetables.

Rice flour roll (Fun guen) is egg-roll shaped, with a thicker rice-flour covering; its appearance is white, not transparent, and it is filled with roast pork, bean sprouts, and Chinese vegetables.

There is also an assortment of buns (bow) that are made of rice flour mixed with wheat flour. They are round, filled with different ingredients and steamed rather than baked as bread is.

There is a roast pork bun (Char shu bow), a peanut butter bun (Jeel yim bow), a black sugar bun (Dow sar bow), a shredded coconut bun (Year see bow), and a chicken bun (Gai bow).

The buns are also served as part of the pastry ensemble at Chinese banquets. Steamed sponge cake is still a third pastry so served. It was served at the Lee Restaurant Anniversary Banquet.

MEAT PATTIES (SHU MEI)

¼ pound ground pork
1 teaspoon cornstarch
4 water chestnuts
¼ cup bamboo shoots

¼ teaspoon salt
¼ teaspoon sugar
dash of pepper
6 pieces wonton skin

Mix ground pork and cornstarch. Mince water chestnuts and bamboo shoots. Mix all ingredients. Fill the 6 pieces of wonton skin so that there are 6 dumplings. Put a little oil on the bottom of a dish and place patties in the dish. Cover and steam for 25 minutes.

NOTE: Serve with haisein sauce (see Guide to Chinese Ingredients).

STEAMED SPONGE CAKE (GAY DON GO)

6 eggs
1½ cups granulated or
    confectionary sugar

2 cups flour
½ teaspoon baking powder

Separate eggs and beat whites and sugar until stiff (about 15 minutes). Add egg yolks and beat for 5 minutes. Sift flour and baking powder together and mix thoroughly with the eggs and sugar. Put mixture in a lightly greased pan, cover and steam for 25 minutes. Cut into 1- or 2-inch squares and serve hot or cold.

DESSERTS

In addition to pastries, Chinese restaurants in America serve fortune cakes, probably an American invention, and spiced kumquats.

Soups (Tong)

When Americans think of Chinese soups they think of wonton and egg drop soup. These two soups are served in every Chinese restaurant in America and have been frozen and canned for home consumption. The Chinese, however, only have wonton soup for lunch or for snacks but never with dinner. Egg drop soup is seldom found in Chinese homes. In Chinese homes, a large common bowl of soup is placed at the center of the table and one dips into it with his porcelain spoon at any point in the meal. Since water is not served at the meal and tea is not generally served until the end, the soup acts as a beverage. Chinese soups, because they are made with generous amounts of vegetables, can be considered one of the vegetable courses of the meal. For example, if you were serving water cress soup (Sy yang choy tong) you may give each person a bowl of soup and then leave the water cress on the table as one of the vegetables. This can be done with a number of the recipes given in this chapter such as bean curd soup (Dow foo tong), hairy melon soup (Jeet quar tong), chicken with lettuce soup (Gai yang sang choy tong) and beef and green cabbage soup (Guy choy ngow tong).

Bird's nest soup (Yeen wor tong) is fascinating to most Americans. It is not made from the mud and twigs of a whole nest as one might infer from the name, but from a gelatinous substance which is a mixture of small fishes and the saliva which the swallow uses to make its nest. Bird's nest is bought in dried, porous, ground form in boxes. It has very little taste of its own but it enhances the flavor and texture of other ingredients which are cooked together with it.

WONTON SOUP (WONTON TONG)

This is the most popular soup served in Chinese restaurants and is easy to make, once you have mastered the art of wrapping the wontons. Wonton skins can be bought at any Chinese grocery store. The filling can be varied by using shrimps and minced Chinese mushrooms (dung goo) with the pork.

⅛ pound ground pork	1 beaten egg
⅛ teaspoon salt	12 pieces wonton skin
¼ teaspoon monosodium glutamate	4 cups chicken broth

Mix pork, salt and monosodium glutamate. Fold into pieces of wonton and seal with egg. Boil wontons in 1 quart of water for 5 minutes. Remove wontons and run cold water over them. Heat chicken broth and add wontons.

INSTRUCTIONS FOR FOLDING WONTON

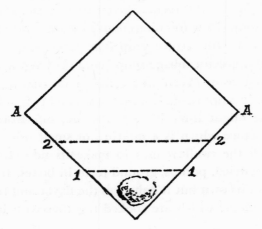

Place a piece of meat (½ in. square) on 1 corner of the wonton skin. Fold at "1" and then "2." Moisten the two corners "A" and "A" with egg and seal them together.

EGG DROP SOUP (DON FAR TONG)

Customers are always fascinated by this soup and are curious as to how it is made. Be sure to pour the egg in very, very slowly. Otherwise you will not get delicate little egg drops. Don far means egg drop.

½ beaten egg
1 quart water
1 tablespoon monosodium
   glutamate

½ teaspoon salt
½ teaspoon sugar
3 tablespoons cornstarch
   mixed with ½ cup water

Beat 1 egg and keep half of it. Add 1 teaspoon water. Bring 1 quart of water to boil and add monosodium glutamate, salt and sugar. Add cornstarch paste. Remove from stove. Pour the beaten egg into the water slowly and keep stirring.

For Tomato Egg Drop Soup (Fon Care Don Far Tong), add ½ cup mashed canned tomatoes to boiling water with other ingredients.

BEAN CURD SOUP (DOW FOO TONG)

A delicate and tasty soup which is very easy to make.

1 brick bean curd (dow foo)
⅛ pound pork
¼ pound Chinese celery cabbage (bok choy)
2 water chestnuts
2 tablespoons bamboo shoots
½ teaspoon monosodium glutamate
½ teaspoon salt (or to taste)
½ teaspoon sugar
1 quart water
1 egg

Slice pork across the grain into thin slices. Slice bean curds into 1-inch squares, celery cabbage into 1-inch pieces, and water chestnuts and bamboo shoots into thin slices. Add all ingredients except egg to 1 quart boiling water. Boil for 10 minutes. Remove from stove and poach egg for three minutes.

CHINESE GREEN CABBAGE SOUP (GUY CHOY NGOW TONG)

¼ pound flank steak (ngow)
½ pound Chinese green cabbage (guy choy)
¼ teaspoon sherry
¼ teaspoon cornstarch
¼ teaspoon soy sauce
¼ teaspoon oil
1 quart water
½ teaspoon monosodium glutamate
½ teaspoon salt (or to taste)
½ teaspoon sugar

Slice steak across the grain into thin slices. Slice green cabbage into thin slices. Mix steak, sherry, cornstarch, soy sauce and oil. Bring water to a boil. Add cabbage, monosodium glutamate, salt and sugar and boil for 10 minutes. Remove from stove and add steak. Stir for 3 minutes.

WATER CRESS SOUP (SY YANG CHOY TONG)

1 bunch water cress (sy yang choy)	½ teaspoon monosodium glutamate
⅛ pound pork	½ teaspoon salt
1 quart water	½ teaspoon sugar
	1 egg

Wash water cress and drain. Slice pork across the grain into thin slices. Bring water to boil. Add all ingredients except egg and boil for 10 minutes. Remove from stove. Poach egg on top of the soup.

HAIRY MELON SOUP (JEET QUAR TONG)

Jeet quar is in the squash family and is seldom served in a Chinese restaurant. It makes a wonderfully light and refreshing soup.

½ pound hairy melon (jeet quar)	1 teaspoon monosodium glutamate
⅛ pound pork	½ teaspoon salt or to taste
1 quart water	½ teaspoon sugar
	1 egg

Peel melon. Slice lengthwise first, then into 1-inch pieces. Slice pork across the grain into thin slices. Bring water to a boil. Add all ingredients except egg and boil for 10 minutes. Remove from stove. Poach egg on top of the soup.

NOTE: You may vary Jeet Quar Tong by adding ⅛ pound gong yu chee (dried scallops) or ⅛ pound chung choy (salted cabbage).

WINTER MELON SOUP (DUNG QUAR JUNG)

Dung quar jung should be served only on special occasions or banquets because it involves so much work. The soup is cooked right inside the melon itself and it is served with the melon as the serving bowl.

1 winter melon (dung quar) about 12 pounds	1 can lotus seeds (lien jee)
½ pound water chestnuts	1 cup 100 Unities (baak haap) optional
½ cup bamboo shoots	¾ teaspoon salt or to taste
1 cup Chinese mushrooms (dung goo)	2 tablespoons monosodium glutamate
½ pound boned chicken breast	1 teaspoon sugar
½ pound boned roasting duck	1 can Chinese white mushrooms (seen gwoo)
⅛ pound Smithfield ham	

Dice water chestnuts, bamboo shoots, mushrooms, chicken breast, duck and ham into ½" cubes. Wash the outside of the melon. Cut across the top of the melon about 2 inches below the top to make a cover. Remove all the seeds. Put all the ingredients into the melon except the ham. Pour water in up to 1 inch from the top. Put the whole melon on a pan so it will not tip over. Put into a large steamer. Cover the melon with the top that was cut off. Steam for 3 hours. Check the pot occasionally to make sure that there is enough water in the steamer. Garnish with ham before serving.

See p. 75 for a description of the banquet version.

WINTER MELON SOUP (DUNG QUAR TONG)

This is a simplified version of Dung Quar Jung

1 pound winter melon
  (dung quar)
2 quarts water
1 teaspoon monosodium
  glutamate
½ teaspoon salt or to taste

½ teaspoon sugar
2 tablespoons cornstarch
  mixed with ¼ cup water
⅛ pound minced Smithfield
  ham

Remove seeds from dung quar. Cut into three-inch squares with the skin. Boil in 2 quarts of water for 40 minutes. Remove but keep the water. Scoop off the meat from the skin and mash. Add winter melon, monosodium glutamate, salt and sugar to water. Bring to a boil and stir in cornstarch paste. Garnish with Smithfield ham.

MINCED CHICKEN WITH LETTUCE SOUP
(GAI YUNG SANG CHOY TONG)

2 cups lettuce (sang choy)
¼ pound boned chicken (gai)
1 quart water
½ teaspoon sugar
½ teaspoon salt or to taste

1 teaspoon monosodium
  glutamate
1 beaten egg white
2 tablespoons minced
  Smithfield ham

Slice lettuce into strips ⅛" x 1". Mince chicken very finely, first with the sharp end of the knife, then with the back of the knife so that it becomes very finely minced (gai yung). Put into ½ cup water and stir well with fork. Remove the tendons. Drain. Bring water to a boil and add sugar, salt, monosodium glutamate and lettuce. When the water begins to boil again, remove from stove and add chicken and egg white. Stir. Garnish with Smithfield ham.

BIRD'S NEST SOUP (GAI YUNG YEEN WOR)

Bird's nest is a misnomer for this soup, because it is actually the secretions of the swallow which holds the nest together rather than the nest itself which is used. Bird's nest comes in a dried form and is sold in boxes at Chinese groceries.

1 cup bird's nest (yeen wor)	2 water chestnuts
¼ pound boned chicken breast (gai)	1 teaspoon cornstarch mixed with 3 tablespoons water
1 quart water	1 beaten egg white
½ teaspoon salt	2 tablespoons minced Smithfield ham
½ teaspoon sugar	
1 teaspoon monosodium glutamate	

Soak bird's nest for 3 hours in cold water. Drain. Boil in 1 quart of water for 15 minutes. Strain out bird's nest and run cool water through it. Pick out all the feathers and dirt. Mince chicken breast very finely, first with the sharp end of the knife, then with the back of the knife so that it becomes very finely minced (gai yung). Mince water chestnuts. Put minced chicken into ½ cup water and stir well with a fork and remove the tendons. Drain. Bring 1 quart of water to boil. Add bird's nest, salt, sugar, monosodium glutamate and water chestnuts. Simmer for 15 minutes. Stir in cornstarch paste and remove from stove. Add minced chicken and egg white. Stir. Garnish with Smithfield ham.

CORN SOUP (GAI YUNG SOOK MEI)

¼ pound boned chicken
  breast (gai)
1 can creamed corn (sook mei)
½ teaspoon salt
½ teaspoon sugar

1 teaspoon monosodium
  glutamate
1 cup water
1 teaspoon cornstarch mixed
  with 3 tablespoons water

1 beaten egg white

Mince chicken breast very finely first with the sharp end of
the knife then with the back of the knife so that it becomes
very finely minced (gai yung). Put into ½ cup water and stir
well with fork. Remove the tendons. Drain. Mix corn, salt,
sugar, monosodium glutamate and water. Bring to a boil.
Add cornstarch paste and remove from stove. Add minced
chicken and egg white. Stir.

Seafood

Fish is one of China's most important staples because of its extensive coast line, rivers, enormous lakes, canals, and man-made fishponds. The making of fish nets is said to have begun as early as 3000 B.C. in China, and slips of bamboo with carved forms of pictograms recorded the fact that people caught fish with the use of pole, line and bait sometime between 1533 and 1027 B.C. The Chinese are also supposed to have been the first to keep goldfish as domesticated pets.

Fish stories are popular the world over, and China is no exception. Whether these stories are true or not makes no difference; they are at least often told and retold. There is a village in China in which it is told that men go fishing in the evenings when there is a full moon. One side of the boat is painted white, and when the moonlight is reflected in the water, the fishes are so fascinated that they jump right out of the water and into the boat. There is another village where a string is tied to the leg of a bird and when the bird catches a fish the fisherman merely has to pull the bird in and remove the fish from its bill.

In art fish symbolizes wealth and abundance because the

Chinese word for fish, *Yu,* is pronounced the same way as the word for superfluity. Because its reproductive powers are so immense, the fish is also a symbol of regeneration. It is greatly admired for its swift, darting movements and perseverance in swimming upstream and in this connection it signifies freedom from all restraints as it moves where it will, and Buddha-hood fully emancipated knows no restrictions. The significance as a symbol of freedom from earthly restraint is the reason why fish is always served at a death banquet, held in honor of the dead on the day of his burial.

The Chinese love fresh fish, so much so that in China they often buy them alive and keep them swimming in vats until needed for use. Some Chinese stores keep fish alive in tanks. Fishes which make good Chinese dishes are: carp, sea bass, mullet, shad, butterfish, perch, and pike. Shellfish such as shrimps, prawns, lobsters, clams, oysters, abalone, and scallops are also very popular although normally abalone is eaten canned, and clams, oysters and scallops are dried. Dried scallops are typically used for making soup.

In cooking fish the Chinese way the secret is in defishing or deodorizing the fish. This is simply done with the use of either vinegar, ginger, scallion or wine, or a combination of these ingredients, as directed in the following recipes.

LOBSTER CANTONESE (CHOW LUNG HAR)

1¼-pound lobster (lung har)	3 teaspoons cornstarch mixed with 4 tablespoons water
1 teaspoon black beans (dow see)	¼ teaspoon sugar
½ teaspoon salt	¼ teaspoon monosodium glutamate
1 clove crushed garlic	dash of pepper
½ pound ground pork	1 tablespoon oil
1½ cups water	

1 egg

Have butcher clean and cut up the live lobster into 8 pieces. Soak black beans in cold water for 10 minutes. Drain. Using a high flame, heat a well-greased frying pan and add salt and garlic. Add beans and pork and stir and cook until pork turns white (chow). Add water and lobster. Cover and cook for 5 minutes. Add cornstarch paste, sugar, monosodium glutamate and pepper. Remove from stove. Sprinkle oil on top, add egg and stir.

Shrimp With Lobster Sauce (Foo Yung Har Kow), a famous dish, is a shrimp variation of the popular Lobster Cantonese. Substitute ½ pound cleaned shrimp (har) cut halfway through (kow) for the lobster and omit black beans.

STEAMED LOBSTER (JING LUNG HAR)

1 lobster (lung har)   2 tablespoons melted butter

Cut lobster spinally into 10 pieces. Reassemble in a Pyrex dish. Cover dish and steam for 4 minutes (jing). Pour melted butter over lobster.

STEAMED LOBSTER WITH SALTED EGG
(YOUNG LUNG HAR)

1¼-pound lobster (lung har)	½ teaspoon sugar
1 ounce Chinese mushrooms	1 teaspoon monosodium
(dung goo)	glutamate
4 water chestnuts	1 teaspoon sherry
1 salted egg (hom don)	2 tablespoons oil
¼ pound ground pork	½ teaspoon cornstarch mixed
1 teaspoon salt	with 3 tablespoons water

Cut lobster spinally into 10 pieces. Reassemble in a Pyrex dish. Soak mushrooms for ½ hour in cold water. Drain. Mince water chestnuts and mushrooms very finely. Separate egg. Mix egg white, pork, water chestnuts, mushrooms, salt, sugar, monosodium glutamate, sherry, oil and cornstarch paste. Spread mixture on top of lobster (young). Break egg yolk and spread on top. Cover and steam for 20 minutes.

FRIED SHRIMP WITH CHINESE VEGETABLES
(CHOW HAR KOW)

½ pound shrimp (har)
½ egg white
2 tablespoons flour
¼ pound Chinese celery cabbage (bok choy)
1 ounce bamboo shoots
8 water chestnuts
½ teaspoon salt or to taste
1 clove garlic

12 snow pea pods
¼ cup water
1 teaspoon cornstarch mixed with 3 tablespoons water
¼ teaspoon sugar
¼ teaspoon monosodium glutamate
dash of pepper

Clean shrimp. Split the back by cutting halfway through to get a fuller shrimp when fried (kow). Mix egg white and flour. Dip shrimp in this batter. Deep-fry in boiling oil. Shrimp will float when done. Cut celery cabbage diagonally. Slice bamboo shoots and water chestnuts thinly. Using a high flame, heat a well-greased frying pan and add salt and garlic. Stir-fry for ½ minute. Add celery cabbage, bamboo shoots, water chestnuts and snow pea pods and stir and cook for 1 minute (chow). Add water. Cover and cook for 2 minutes. Add shrimp, cornstarch paste, sugar, monosodium glutamate and pepper. Stir.

PAN-FRIED SHRIMP (CHOW HAR LOOK)

¾ pound large shrimp (har)
2 tablespoons oil
¾ teaspoon salt
1 clove garlic
1 teaspoon chopped ginger
  root
¼ cup water
2 tablespoons catsup

1 teaspoon sherry
1 sliced scallion
1 teaspoon cornstarch mixed
  with 3 tablespoons water
2 teaspoons sugar
1 teaspoon monosodium
  glutamate
dash of pepper

Remove head and legs of shrimp and slit shell to remove intestine but leave shell on (har look). Using a high flame, heat frying pan and add 1 tablespoon oil and ¼ teaspoon salt. Brown garlic clove. Fry shrimps on both sides, 2 minutes on each side (chow). Remove and set aside. Heat pan again and add 1 tablespoon oil, ½ teaspoon salt, and ginger root. Add water, fried shrimp, catsup, sherry, scallion and bring to a boil. Add cornstarch paste, sugar, monosodium glutamate and pepper and cook and stir for ½ minute.

NOTE: The trick here is to remove the shell in your mouth.

BUTTERFLY SHRIMP (WOR TEAP HAR)

12 large shrimp (har)
12 thin slices Smithfield ham
  1½" x ½"
1 large onion
1 egg
4 tablespoons flour
12 1½" slices bacon
½ teaspoon salt
1 clove garlic

½ cup water
¼ teaspoon catsup
2 tablespoons Worcestershire
  sauce
3 teaspoons sugar
dash of pepper
2 teaspoons cornstarch mixed
  with 4 tablespoons water

Remove shell and intestinal vein from shrimp. Split by cutting halfway through and flatten out. Slice onion into half rings. Place a piece of ham on each shrimp. Mix egg and flour. Dip bacon into batter. Place dipped bacon over ham and shrimp. Fry on bacon side for 3 minutes in well-greased frying pan. Turn over and fry 3 minutes more. Remove and set aside. Stir-fry onion for 2 minutes. Arrange onions on bottom of serving dish and cover with fried shrimp. Using a high flame, heat a well-greased frying pan and add salt. Brown garlic. Add water, catsup, Worcestershire sauce, sugar and pepper. Bring to boil and add cornstarch paste. Pour over shrimp.

Wor teap means butterfly.

SHRIMP WITH TOMATO SAUCE (CARE JUP HAR)

½ pound shrimp (har)
½ teaspoon salt
1 clove crushed garlic
¼ cup water
1½ teaspoons sugar
dash of pepper
¼ teaspoon monosodium
    glutamate

4 tablespoons catsup
    (care jup)
1½ teaspoons cornstarch
    mixed with 3 tablespoons
    water

Remove shell and intestinal vein from shrimp. Split by cutting halfway through. Boil for 2 minutes. Using a high flame, heat a well-greased frying pan and add salt and garlic. Stir-fry for ½ minute. Add water, sugar, pepper, monosodium glutamate, catsup and shrimp. Bring to boil and add cornstarch paste. Stir.

SHRIMP WITH BEAN SPROUTS (ARE CHOY HAR)

½ pound shrimp (har)
½ pound bean sprouts
  (are choy)
1 clove garlic
½ teaspoon salt
¼ cup water

1 slice ginger root
1 teaspoon cornstarch mixed
  with 3 tablespoons water
¼ teaspoon sugar
¼ teaspoon monosodium
  glutamate

dash of pepper

Remove shell and intestinal vein from shrimp. Split by cutting halfway through. Boil for 2 minutes. Wash bean sprouts in several changes of water. Drain. Using a high flame, heat a well-greased frying pan and add garlic and salt. Stir-fry the bean sprouts for ½ minute. Add water and ginger root. Cover and cook for 2 minutes. Add shrimp, cornstarch paste, sugar, monosodium glutamate and pepper. Cook and stir for ½ minute.

BATTER-FRIED SHRIMP (JOW HAR)

½ pound shrimp (har)   ½ of 1 egg white
        2 tablespoons flour

Remove shell and intestinal vein from shrimp. Split by cutting halfway through. Mix egg white and flour. Dip shrimp in this batter. Deep-fry in boiling oil (jow). Shrimp will float when done.

FRIED SHRIMP (JOW HAR)

12 shrimp (har)
¼ teaspoon salt

¼ teaspoon soy sauce
½ teaspoon sherry

        2 teaspoons cornstarch

Peel and clean shrimp, leaving the tail on. Split halfway through the back. Mix salt, soy sauce, and sherry. Marinate shrimp for 10 minutes. Coat with cornstarch. Deep-fry (jow). Shrimp will float when done.

CURRIED SHRIMP (GAR LAY HAR)

¾ pound shrimp (har)
1 large onion
3 tablespoons curry (gar lay)
½ cup water
¾ teaspoon salt
1 teaspoon sherry

1½ teaspoons cornstarch mixed with 4 tablespoons water
1 teaspoon sugar
1 teaspoon monosodium glutamate
dash of pepper

Remove shell and intestinal vein from shrimp. Split by cutting halfway through. Boil for 2 minutes. Slice onion into half rings. Using a high flame, heat a frying pan without grease. Stir-fry onions for 2 minutes. Reduce heat to medium. Add curry powder and cook, stirring constantly, for 2 minutes. Add water, salt, sherry, and shrimp. Increase heat to high and bring mixture to a boil. Add cornstarch paste, sugar, monosodium glutamate and pepper. Stir.

SHRIMP WITH CHINESE CABBAGE (BOK CHOY HAR)

½ pound shrimp (har)
½ pound Chinese celery cabbage (bok choy)
1 clove garlic
¼ cup water
1 teaspoon cornstarch mixed with 3 tablespoons water

¼ teaspoon sugar
½ teaspoon salt
1 teaspoon soy sauce
¼ teaspoon monosodium glutamate
1 slice ginger root
dash of pepper

Remove shell and intestinal vein from shrimp. Split by cutting halfway through. Boil for 2 minutes. Cut celery cabbage diagonally in pieces 1½" long. Using a high flame, heat a well-greased frying pan and brown garlic. Stir-fry celery cab-

bage for ½ minute. Add water, cover and cook for 2 minutes.
Add shrimp, cornstarch paste, sugar, salt, soy sauce, monosodium glutamate, ginger root and pepper. Cook and stir for
½ minute.

DICED SHRIMP WITH CHINESE VEGETABLES
(CHOW HAR YUN)

¼ pound shrimp (har)
2 cups Chinese celery cabbage
  (bok choy)
8 water chestnuts
¼ cup bamboo shoots
12 snow pea pods
½ teaspoon salt
1 garlic clove
¼ cup frozen peas

¼ cup button mushrooms
¼ cup water
1½ teaspoons cornstarch
  mixed with 3 tablespoons
  water
¼ teaspoon sugar
¼ teaspoon monosodium
  glutamate

Remove shell and intestinal vein from shrimp. Boil for 2
minutes. Dice shrimp, celery cabbage, water chestnuts, bamboo shoots, snow pea pods (yun). Using a high flame, heat a
well-greased frying pan and add salt. Brown garlic. Add
celery cabbage, water chestnuts, bamboo shoots, snow pea
pods, frozen peas, mushrooms and stir-fry for ½ minute
(chow). Add water. Cover and cook 2 minutes. Add shrimp,
cornstarch paste, sugar and monosodium glutamate. Stir.

STEAMED FISH (JING YU)

1 pound sea bass, porgy or
  butterfish (yu)
2 teaspoons brown bean sauce
  (mien see)
1 teaspoon shredded ginger
  root
½ sliced scallion

4 tablespoons water
½ teaspoon salt
¼ teaspoon sugar
¼ teaspoon monosodium
  glutamate
dash pepper
1 teaspoon soy sauce

2 tablespoons oil

Mash brown bean sauce. Place fish in a Pyrex dish. Mix all other ingredients except 1 tablespoon oil and pour over fish. Cover and steam for 12 minutes (jing). Pour remaining 1 tablespoon oil over fish before serving.

STEAMED FISH WITH MEAT SHREDS AND CHINESE MUSHROOMS (JING YU)

1 **pound porgy or sea bass (yu)**	1 **teaspoon soy sauce**
1 **ounce Chinese mushrooms (dung goo)**	1 **teaspoon monosodium glutamate**
⅛ **pound fresh ham**	¾ **teaspoon salt**
2 **teaspoons chopped ginger root**	½ **teaspoon cornstarch mixed with 3 tablespoons water**
½ **sliced scallion**	**dash of pepper**

2 **tablespoons oil**

Soak mushrooms for ½ hour in cold water to soften. Drain. Shred mushrooms and fresh ham. Place fish in Pyrex dish. Mix all other ingredients except 1 tablespoon oil. Pour over fish. Cover and steam for 18 minutes (jing). Sprinkle remaining 1 tablespoon oil over fish before serving.

FRIED FISH WITH BEAN CURDS (DOW FOO JEEN YU)

2 **bean curds (dow foo)**	1 **teaspoon soy sauce**
2 **tablespoons oil**	1 **teaspoon sherry**
1 **teaspoon salt**	1 **teaspoon sugar**
1 **slice ginger root shredded**	1 **teaspoon monosodium glutamate**
1 **pound sea bass or porgy (yu)**	**dash of pepper**
1 **cup water**	
1 **sliced scallion**	
1½ **teaspoons cornstarch mixed with 3 tablespoons water**	

Cut bean curds into 8 pieces. Deep-fry until light brown. Using a high flame, heat a frying pan with 2 tablespoons oil and ¼ teaspoon salt. Fry fish 4 minutes on each side (jeen). Remove and set aside. Heat pan again with 1 tablespoon oil, ¾ teaspoon salt and ginger. Add water and bean curds. Place the fish on top and garnish with sliced scallion. Cover and cook for 4 minutes. Remove fish and bean curds and set aside. Add cornstarch paste, soy sauce, sherry, sugar, monosodium glutamate and pepper. Pour over fish.

STEAMED FISH WITH BEAN CURDS (DOW FOO JING YU)

2 bean curds (dow foo)	½ teaspoon salt
1 pound sea bass, porgy or butterfish (yu)	dash of pepper
	¼ teaspoon sugar
2 teaspoons brown bean sauce (mien see)	¼ teaspoon monosodium glutamate
1 teaspoon shredded ginger root	¼ teaspoon soy sauce
	4 tablespoons water
1 quarter scallion diced	2 tablespoons oil

Cut bean curds into 8 pieces. Place fish in Pyrex dish. Crush brown bean sauce. Mix brown bean sauce, ginger root, scallion, salt, pepper, sugar, monosodium glutamate, soy sauce, water and 1 tablespoon oil. Pour mixture over fish. Place the bean curds on the side of the fish. Cover and steam for 12 minutes (jing). Pour the 1 remaining tablespoon of oil over fish before serving.

FRIED BONED FISH WITH CHINESE VEGETABLES (YU PEEN)

1 pound boned pike (yu)	2 tablespoons oil
1 tablespoon cornstarch	1 clove garlic
¾ teaspoon salt	12 snow pea pods
1 teaspoon sherry	¼ cup water
2 tablespoons bamboo shoots	¼ teaspoon monosodium
3 water chestnuts	glutamate
¼ pound Chinese celery	¼ teaspoon sugar
cabbage (bok choy)	dash of pepper

8 slices ginger root

Slice fish diagonally into slices of ⅛" thickness (peen). Mix cornstarch, ¼ teaspoon salt and sherry. Dip fish in this. Slice bamboo shoots, water chestnuts and celery cabbage into ⅛" slices. Using a high flame, heat a well-greased frying pan and add 1 tablespoon oil and ¼ teaspoon salt. Brown garlic. Stir-fry celery cabbage, bamboo shoots, water chestnuts and snow pea pods for 1 minute. Add water, monosodium glutamate, sugar and pepper. Cover and cook for 2 minutes. Remove and set aside. Heat pan again with 1 tablespoon oil, ¼ teaspoon salt and ginger root. Add fish and cook and stir carefully for ½ minute. Add vegetables and mix.

SWEET AND SOUR FISH (TIEM SHUEN YU)

1 pound sea bass (yu)	¼ cup vinegar
½ green pepper	5 tablespoons sugar
1 ring pineapple	1 teaspoon soy sauce
1 carrot	¼ teaspoon monosodium
1 egg	glutamate
5 tablespoons flour	dash of pepper
¾ teaspoon salt	3 teaspoons cornstarch mixed
5 slices ginger root	with 6 tablespoons water
1½ cups water	

Shred green pepper, carrot and pineapple. Mix egg and flour. Dip fish in batter. Deep-fry in boiling oil 4 minutes on each side. Remove and place in serving dish. Using a high flame, heat a well-greased pan and add salt and ginger. Add water, vinegar, green pepper, carrot, pineapple, sugar, soy sauce, monosodium glutamate and pepper. Bring mixture to a boil. Stir in cornstarch paste and pour over fish.

For Sweet And Sour Shrimp (Tiem Shuen Har), substitute 1 pound cleaned shrimp for sea bass. (Tiem shuen means sweet and sour.)

FRIED FISH IN VEGETABLES (HUNG SHEW YU)

1 pound sea bass (yu)
⅛ pound pork
2 ounces Chinese mushrooms (dung goo)
2 cups Chinese celery cabbage (bok choy)
2 tablespoons bamboo shoots
1 beaten egg
5 tablespoons flour
1 teaspoon shredded ginger root

1½ cups water
¾ teaspoon salt
1 teaspoon sugar
½ teaspoon monosodium glutamate
1 teaspoon soy sauce
1 teaspoon sherry
pinch of golden needles (gum jum)
2 teaspoons cornstarch mixed with 4 tablespoons water

Soak mushrooms in cold water for ½ hour to soften. Drain. Shred pork, mushrooms, celery cabbage, bamboo shoots into pieces 1½" x ⅛" x ⅛". Mix egg and flour. Dip fish in batter. Deep-fry in boiling oil for 4 minutes on each side, making sure that the fish is completely immersed in oil. Drain. Using a high flame, heat a well-greased frying pan and add ginger root. Stir-fry pork until it becomes white. Add celery cabbage, mushrooms, bamboo shoots and water. Cover and cook for 2 minutes. Add salt, sugar, monosodium glutamate, soy sauce, sherry, golden needles and cornstarch paste. Cook and stir for ½ minute. Pour over fish.

FISH KOW (YU KOW)

1 pound boned pike (yu)
3 tablespoons flour
1 teaspoon sherry
1 egg white
¼ pound Chinese celery cabbage (bok choy)
1 ounce bamboo shoots
8 water chestnuts
½ teaspoon salt or to taste
1 clove garlic

12 snow pea pods
¼ cup water
1 teaspoon cornstarch mixed with 3 tablespoons water
¼ teaspoon sugar
¼ teaspoon monosodium glutamate
1 teaspoon shredded ginger root
dash of pepper

Cut fish into 1″ squares (kow). Mix flour, sherry and egg white. Dip fish into this batter. Deep-fry in boiling oil for 5 minutes. Cut celery cabbage diagonally. Slice bamboo shoots and water chestnuts thinly. Using a high flame, heat a well-greased frying pan and add salt. Brown garlic clove. Add celery cabbage, bamboo shoots, water chestnuts and snow pea pods and stir-fry for 1 minute. Add water. Cover and cook for 2 minutes. Add fish, cornstarch paste, sugar, monosodium glutamate, ginger root and pepper. Stir.

SEA BASS WITH TOMATOES (FON CARE YU)

1 pound sea bass (yu)
2 large tomatoes (fon care)
1 scallion
1 teaspoon salt
1 clove garlic
1 cup water
2 teaspoons cornstarch mixed with 3 tablespoons water

1 teaspoon soy sauce
1 teaspoon sherry
2 teaspoons sugar
1 slice ginger root
½ teaspoon monosodium glutamate
dash of pepper

Cut tomatoes into 1″ squares and scallion into 1″ pieces. Using a high flame, heat a well-greased frying pan and add ¼ teaspoon salt. Brown fish on both sides. Remove and set aside. Heat and grease pan again and add garlic and ¾ teaspoon salt. Stir-fry for ½ minute. Add water. Bring to a boil. Add fish, scallion, and tomatoes and cook for 3 minutes. Remove fish, scallion and tomatoes. Add cornstarch paste, soy sauce, sherry, sugar, ginger root, monosodium glutamate and pepper. Stir. Pour over fish.

Poultry

Poultry, especially chicken, is almost always served to dinner guests in China. Not only is chicken delicious and rather easy to prepare, it also can be completely consumed in one meal so that there is no problems of spoilage as in slaughtering a cow or a pig. Aside from the practical aspects there is much symbolism attached to birds. The cock is the incarnation of *Yang* which represents all the warm and positive elements of universal life. The symbol of felicity is given to ducks whereas the pigeon is noted for its filial duty to its mate and offspring and for its benevolence. At a wedding banquet one will find all three of these birds served in the course of the three-hour meal symbolizing the attributes of each of these birds which will add up to a happy marriage.

The Chinese like freshly killed chickens because they are more tasty than the frozen kind. In some cities in the United States the only place to buy freshly killed fowl is at Kosher chicken markets. A number of the following recipes call for chicken breasts and the easiest thing to do is to simply buy chicken breasts instead of the whole chicken. In a number of the following recipes, chicken is boiled. This is an excellent way to use any leftover cooked chicken.

DICED CHICKEN WITH VEGETABLES (GAI DING)

½ pound boned chicken (gai)
¼ cup almonds
½ cup canned mushrooms
½ pound Chinese celery cabbage (bok choy)
4 water chestnuts
½ cup bamboo shoots
12 snow pea pods
¼ cup celery

¼ teaspoon salt or to taste
¼ cup water
1 teaspoon cornstarch mixed with 3 tablespoons water
dash of pepper
¼ teaspoon sugar
½ teaspoon monosodium glutamate

Deep-fry almonds for 3 minutes and allow to cool. Boil chicken for 20 minutes. Allow to cool. Dice chicken and all vegetables into ¼" x ¼" pieces (ding). Using a high flame, heat a well-greased pan and add salt. Add mushrooms, celery cabbage, water chestnuts, bamboo shoots, snow pea pods and celery. Stir-fry for ½ minute. Add ¼ cup water. Cover and cook for 2 minutes. Add chicken and stir. Add cornstarch paste, pepper, sugar, monosodium glutamate and cook and stir for ½ minute. Top with almonds before serving.

CHICKEN WITH HAM (YEEN YANG GAI)

1 pound boned chicken (gai)
¼ pound Smithfield ham
¼ teaspoon salt
¼ cup water
1 teaspoon cornstarch mixed with 3 tablespoons water

¼ teaspoon sugar
½ teaspoon monosodium glutamate

Boil chicken for 20 minutes. Allow to cool. Slice chicken and ham into 1½" x 1" pieces. Place in serving dish, alternating ham and chicken. Using a high flame, heat a well-greased frying pan and add salt. Add water and bring to boil. Add cornstarch paste, sugar, monosodium glutamate and stir. Pour over ham and chicken.

CHICKEN COOKED IN CHINESE MUSHROOM SAUCE
(DUNG GOO WAT GAI)

½ spring chicken (gai)
1 cup Chinese mushrooms
  (dung goo)
¼ cup bamboo shoots
4 water chestnuts
2 scallions
1 tablespoon soy sauce
5 thin slices ginger root
1 teaspoon salt

2½ cups water
½ teaspoon sugar
1 teaspoon monosodium
  glutamate
dash of pepper
pinch golden needles (gum
  jum) optional
2 teaspoons cornstarch mixed
  with 3 tablespoons water

Soak mushrooms for ½ hour in cold water to soften. Drain. Slice mushrooms and bamboo shoots into ⅛-inch strips. Slice water chestnuts and scallions finely. Rub soy sauce into chicken. Deep-fry for 2 minutes on each side. Using a high flame, heat a well-greased frying pan and add ginger root and salt. Add water, mushrooms, scallions, water chestnuts, bamboo shoots, sugar, monosodium glutamate, pepper and golden needles. Place chicken on top of this. Reduce heat to low, cover and cook for 15 minutes (wat). Remove chicken and cut into 1½″ x 1″ pieces and place in serving dish. (You will need either a Chinese knife or a butcher knife.) Add cornstarch paste to liquid in pan and cook and stir for ½ minute. Pour over chicken.

SOY SAUCE COOKED CHICKEN (SEE YOW GAI)

4–5 pound roasting chicken (gai)	2½ quarts water
	1 quart soy sauce (see yow)
½ pound sugar	

Bring water to boil. Add soy sauce and sugar. Stir until sugar is dissolved. Add chicken, cover and simmer for 15 minutes.

NOTE: If the soy sauce does not completely cover the chicken, cook one side for 10 minutes, turn chicken and cook for another 10 minutes.

SLICED CHICKEN WITH PINEAPPLE (BOR LOR GAI PEEN)

½ pound boned chicken breast	4 thin slices ginger root
	¼ teaspoon salt
¼ cup Chinese mushrooms (dung goo)	¼ cup water
	1 teaspoon cornstarch mixed with 3 tablespoons water
1 cup Chinese celery cabbage (bok choy)	½ teaspoon sugar
¼ cup bamboo shoots	½ teaspoon salt
4 slices pineapple (bor lor)	½ teaspoon monosodium glutamate
4 water chestnuts	
½ teaspoon soy sauce	

Boil chicken for 20 minutes. Allow to cool. Slice into 1½-inch squares by cutting diagonally (peen). Soak mushrooms for ½ hour in cold water to soften. Drain. Slice celery cabbage diagonally into 1-inch pieces, mushrooms into ⅛-inch strips, bamboo shoots and pineapple into 1-inch pieces and water chestnuts thinly. Using a high flame, heat a well-greased frying pan and add ginger root and salt. Add celery cabbage, mushrooms, bamboo shoots and water chestnuts. Stir-fry for ½ minute. Add water. Cover and cook for 3 minutes. Add chicken and pineapple and bring to a boil. Stir in cornstarch paste, sugar, monosodium glutamate and soy sauce.

DICED CHICKEN WITH WALNUTS (HOP TO GAI DING)

½ pound boned chicken (gai)
¼ cup walnuts (hop to)
½ cup canned mushrooms
½ pound Chinese celery cabbage (bok choy)
4 water chestnuts
¼ cup bamboo shoots
12 snow pea pods

¼ cup celery
¼ teaspoon salt or to taste
¼ cup water
1 teaspoon cornstarch mixed with 3 tablespoons water
¼ teaspoon sugar
½ teaspoon monosodium glutamate

dash of pepper

Boil chicken for 20 minutes. Allow to cool. Deep-fry walnuts for 2 minutes. Allow to cool. Dice chicken and all vegetables in ¼″ cubes (ding). Using a high flame, heat a well-greased frying pan and add salt. Add mushrooms, celery cabbage, water chestnuts, bamboo shoots, snow pea pods and celery. Stir-fry for ½ minute. Add water. Cover and cook for 2 minutes. Add chicken and stir. Add cornstarch paste, sugar, monosodium glutamate and pepper. Cook and stir for ½ minute. Remove from stove and add walnuts.

FRIED CHICKEN CANTONESE (JOW GAI)

½ spring chicken (gai)
¼ cup Chinese mushrooms (dung goo)
½ cup Chinese celery cabbage (bok choy)
¼ cup bamboo shoots
2 water chestnuts
1 tablespoon soy sauce
2 tablespoons sherry

4 thin slices ginger root
¼ teaspoon salt
½ cup water
1 teaspoon cornstarch mixed with 3 tablespoons water
½ teaspoon sugar
½ teaspoon monosodium glutamate
dash of pepper

Soak mushrooms in cold water for ½ hour to soften. Drain. Slice celery cabbage diagonally into ½-inch pieces, bamboo shoots into 1-inch squares, mushrooms into ⅛-inch strips and water chestnuts finely. Rub soy sauce and sherry into the chicken and let it soak for 10 minutes. Deep-fry for 5 minutes on each side (jow). Using a high flame, heat a well-greased frying pan and add ginger root and salt. Add water chestnuts, bamboo shoots, celery cabbage, mushrooms and stir-fry for ½ minute. Add water. Cover and cook for 3 minutes. Add cornstarch paste, sugar, monosodium glutamate and pepper. Cook and stir for ½ minute. Cut chicken into 1½″ x 1″ pieces and place in serving dish. (You will need either a Chinese knife or butcher knife.) Place vegetables on top of chicken.

SWEET AND SOUR CHICKEN BONES
(TIEM SHUEN GAI GWOT)

¼ chicken
¼ cup carrots
¼ cup green pepper
1 slice pineapple
¼ teaspoon salt or to taste
1 clove crushed garlic
½ cup water
¼ cup vinegar

5 tablespoons sugar
1½ teaspoons soy sauce
1 teaspoon monosodium
   glutamate
dash of pepper
2 teaspoons cornstarch mixed
   with 3 tablespoons water

Cut chicken with bones into 1-inch pieces (gai gwot). (You will need either a Chinese knife or butcher knife.) Deep-fry in boiling oil for 5 minutes. Slice carrots diagonally into thin pieces, green pepper into 1-inch squares and pineapple into 1-inch pieces. Using a high flame, heat a well-greased frying pan and add salt and garlic. Add water, vinegar, sugar, soy sauce, monosodium glutamate and pepper. Bring to a boil. Stir in cornstarch paste, carrots, green pepper, pineapple and chicken.

Tiem shuen means sweet and sour.

CHICKEN WINGS WITH OYSTER SAUCE (HO YOW GAI YICK)

8 chicken wings (gai yick)
1 scallion
4 thin slices ginger root
¼ teaspoon salt
4 tablespoons water
4 tablespoon oyster sauce
(ho yow)

1 teaspoon cornstarch mixed
with 2 tablespoons water
½ teaspoon sugar
½ teaspoon monosodium
glutamate
dash of pepper

Cut each chicken wing into 3 pieces. Cut scallion into 1-inch pieces. Using a high flame, heat a well-greased frying pan and add ginger root and salt. Add chicken wings and fry until brown. Add water, oyster sauce and scallion. Cover and simmer for 10 minutes. Add cornstarch paste, sugar, monosodium glutamate and pepper and cook and stir for ½ minute.

CURRIED CHICKEN (GAR LAY GAI)

¼ pound boned chicken (gai)
1 medium size onion
4 tablespoons curry powder
(gar lay)
½ cup water
¼ teaspoon salt

1 teaspoon cornstarch mixed
with 3 tablespoons water
½ teaspoon sugar
½ teaspoon monosodium
glutamate
dash of pepper

Slice chicken into 1-inch squares and onion into half rings. Stir-fry onion for 2 minutes in a very hot well-greased frying pan. Add curry powder, reduce heat to medium and cook for 5 minutes. Add chicken. Stir-fry for 3 minutes. Add water, and salt. Increase heat to high and cook for 4 minutes. Stir in cornstarch paste, sugar, monosodium glutamate and pepper.

STEAMED CHICKEN (JING GAI)

½ spring chicken (gai)
½ cup Chinese mushrooms (dung goo)
¼ cup bamboo shoots
4 water chestnuts
1½ teaspoons oil
½ teaspoon sugar

1 teaspoon soy sauce
½ teaspoon monosodium glutamate
dash of pepper
½ teaspoon cornstarch mixed with 3 tablespoons water

Soak mushrooms in cold water for ½ hour to soften. Drain. Cut into ⅛-inch strips. Chop chicken into 1½″ x 1″ pieces. (You will need either a Chinese knife or butcher knife.) Slice bamboo shoots and water chestnuts into thin slices. Mix all ingredients. Place in dish, cover and steam for 15 minutes (jing).

ONE CHICKEN THREE FLAVORS (YAT GAI SAM MAY)

This is a wonderful way to make a complete dinner with one chicken and come out with three different dishes.

1. The chicken livers and gizzards make soup with dow foo and bok choy. Dow Foo Tong (p. 89).

2. The breasts and other pieces of meat are used to make Moo Goo Gai Peen (p. 121).

3. The bony pieces such as the legs and back are used to make Tiem Shuen Gai Gwot (p. 118).

CHICKEN WITH MUSHROOMS (MOO GOO GAI PEEN)

½ pound boned chicken breast (gai)
½ cup canned mushrooms (moo goo)
½ pound Chinese celery cabbage (bok choy)
¼ cup bamboo shoots
1 stalk celery
4 water chestnuts

¼ teaspoon salt
12 snow pea pods
¼ cup water
1 teaspoon cornstarch mixed with 3 tablespoons water
½ teaspoon monosodium glutamate
dash of pepper
¼ teaspoon sugar

Boil chicken for 20 minutes. Allow it to cool. Slice diagonally into 1½" squares. Slice mushrooms, celery cabbage, celery and bamboo shoots into ½-inch slices and water chestnuts as thinly as possible (peen). Using a high flame, heat a well-greased frying pan and add salt. Add mushrooms, celery cabbage, water chestnuts, bamboo shoots, snow pea pods and celery. Stir-fry for ½ minute. Add water. Cover and cook for 2 minutes. Add chicken, cornstarch paste, monosodium glutamate, pepper and sugar. Stir and cook for ½ minute.

CHICKEN AND SNOW PEAS (SOOT DOW GAI PEEN)

½ pound boned chicken (gai)
¼ cup bamboo shoots
4 water chestnuts
4 slices ginger root
¼ teaspoon salt
¼ cup water
¼ pound snow pea pods (soot dow)

1 teaspoon cornstarch mixed with 3 tablespoons water
½ teaspoon sugar
½ teaspoon monosodium glutamate
1 teaspoon soy sauce
dash of pepper

Slice chicken into 1½-inch squares, bamboo shoots into 1-inch squares and water chestnuts as thinly as possible (peen). Using a high flame, heat a well-greased pan and add ginger root and salt. Stir-fry chicken for 2 minutes. Add water. Cover and cook for 2 minutes. Add snow pea pods, bamboo shoots and water chestnuts. Cover and cook for 1 minute. Stir in cornstarch paste, sugar, monosodium glutamate, soy sauce and pepper.

SLICED CHICKEN WITH PINEAPPLE (BOR LOR GAI PEEN)

¼ pound boned chicken
    breast (gai)
¼ cup Chinese mushrooms
    (dung goo)
1 cup Chinese celery cabbage
    (bok choy)
¼ cup bamboo shoots
3 slices pineapple (bor lor)
4 water chestnuts

4 thin slices ginger root
¼ teaspoon salt
¼ cup water
1 teaspoon cornstarch mixed
    with 3 tablespoons water
½ teaspoon sugar
½ teaspoon monosodium
    glutamate
½ teaspoon soy sauce

Boil chicken for 20 minutes. Allow to cool. Slice into 1½" squares by cutting diagonally (peen). Soak mushrooms for ½ hour in cold water to soften. Drain. Slice celery cabbage diagonally into 1" pieces. Slice mushrooms into ⅛" slices. Slice bamboo shoots and pineapple into 1" pieces and water chestnuts thinly. Using a high flame, heat a well-greased frying pan and add ginger root and salt. Add celery cabbage, mushrooms, bamboo shoots and water chestnuts. Stir-fry for ½ minute. Add ¼ cup water. Cover and cook for 3 minutes. Add chicken and pineapple and bring to boil. Add cornstarch paste, sugar, monosodium glutamate and soy sauce. Stir.

FRIED CHICKEN LIVERS AND GIZZARDS (JOW GAI GONE)

4 chicken livers
4 chicken gizzards } (gai gone)
1 teaspoon soy sauce

¼ teaspoon salt
¼ teaspoon sugar
1 teaspoon sherry

2 tablespoons cornstarch

Cut livers and gizzards into 1-inch squares. Mix soy sauce, salt, sugar and sherry. Marinate livers and gizzards for 5 minutes. Coat with cornstarch. Deep fry (jow). They will float when done.

SQUAB WITH OYSTER SAUCE (HO YOW BOK OPP)

2 squabs (bok opp)
1 teaspoon soy sauce
½ teaspoon salt
2 tablespoons oil
1½ cups water
3 tablespoons oyster sauce
  (ho yow)
1 teaspoon sugar

dash of pepper
1 teaspoon monosodium
  glutamate
1 teaspoon sherry
1½ teaspoons cornstarch
  mixed with 3 tablespoons
  water

Cut the back of the squabs and lay out flat. Rub soy sauce into the squabs. Brown in very hot frying pan with ¼ teaspoon salt and 1 tablespoon oil. Remove and set aside. Heat pan again with ¼ teaspoon salt and 1 tablespoon oil. Add water, oyster sauce, sugar, pepper, monosodium glutamate, sherry and squabs. Cover and cook squabs on each side for 5 minutes. Remove squabs and cut into 1½″ squares. (You will need either a Chinese knife or butcher knife.) Add cornstarch paste to thicken gravy and pour over squab.

MINCED SQUAB WITH ASSORTED VEGETABLES
(BOK OPP SOONG)

1 boned squab (bok opp)
¼ cup Chinese mushrooms
  (dung goo)
1 cup Chinese celery cabbage
  (bok choy)
¼ cup water chestnuts
¼ cup bamboo shoots
¼ cup snow pea pods

½ teaspoon salt
¾ cup water
1 teaspoon cornstarch mixed
  with 3 tablespoons water
½ teaspoon sugar
1 teaspoon monosodium
  glutamate
dash of pepper

Soak mushrooms ½ hour in cold water to soften. Drain. Mince squab and all vegetables (soong). Using a high flame, heat a well-greased frying pan and add salt. Stir-fry all vegetables for ½ minute. Add ½ cup water. Cover and cook for 2 minutes. Remove vegetables and set aside. Stir-fry squab meat for 1 minute. Add ¼ cup water. Cover and cook for 2 minutes. Return vegetables to the pan and add cornstarch paste, sugar, monosodium glutamate and pepper. Cook and stir for ½ minute.

CHINESE FRIED SQUAB (JOW BOK OPP)

2 squabs (bok opp)　　　　　2 teaspoons soy sauce
1 teaspoon sherry

Cut through backs of squabs and place flat in dish. Mix soy sauce and sherry. Marinate squabs for 15 minutes. Deep-fry in boiling oil for 2 minutes (jow). Remove from stove and keep squabs in the oil for 2 minutes. Turn them over and repeat above procedure. Drain.

DUCK WITH POTATOES (SHEE JAI OPP)

5-pound duck (opp)
4 tablespoons soy sauce
¼ cup oil
2 pounds potatoes (shee jai)
2 tablespoons salt
1 tablespoon sugar
dash of pepper
1 teaspoon monosodium
  glutamate

¼ cup nom yee (a spice)
  or
¼ cup brown bean sauce
  (mien see)
1 quart water
2 teaspoons cornstarch mixed
  with 4 tablespoons water

Cut through the back of the duck and clean. Rub 2 table-spoons soy sauce on the duck. Fry duck in ¼ cup oil in a very hot frying pan for 20 minutes turning constantly. Peel potatoes and cut into 2-inch cubes. Mix 2 tablespoons soy sauce, salt, sugar, pepper, monosodium glutamate, nom yee or brown bean sauce, water and potatoes. Bring to a boil and add fried duck. Cover and cook for 10 minutes on medium heat. Turn duck over and cook for another 10 minutes. Remove duck and potatoes and cut duck into 1½″ pieces. (You will need either a Chinese knife or a butcher knife.) Add cornstarch paste to remaining broth and make a gravy. Pour over duck and potatoes.

DUCK WITH PARSLEY (SY WU OPP)

5-pound duck (opp)
½ cup Chinese mushrooms
  (dung goo)
½ cup bamboo shoots
4 tablespoons soy sauce
2 teaspoons salt
2 teaspoons sugar
1 teaspoon monosodium
  glutamate

1 quart water
2 ounces Chinese parsley
2 teaspoons cornstarch mixed
  with 3 tablespoons water
2 tablespoons shredded
  Smithfield ham

Soak mushrooms for ½ hour in cold water to soften. Drain. Shred mushrooms and bamboo shoots. Cut the back of the duck and clean. Rub 2 tablespoons soy sauce on the duck. Deep-fry for 10 minutes. Mix 2 tablespoons soy sauce, salt, sugar, monosodium glutamate and water. Boil duck for 25 minutes on each side. Line serving dish with Chinese parsley and place duck on top. To remaining liquid add mushrooms and bamboo shoots and cook for 5 minutes. Stir in cornstarch paste and pour over duck. Garnish with ham shreds.

For description of banquet version see p. 76.

BRAISED BONELESS DUCK (WOR SHEW OPP)

5-pound duck (opp)
½ cup and 4 tablespoons soy sauce
1 quart water
4 tablespoons salt
3 tablespoons sugar

¼ cup leung leel (a spice)
1 cup flour
2 teaspoons cornstarch mixed with 3 tablespoons water
2 teaspoons crushed almonds
lettuce

Cut through the back of the duck and clean. Rub 4 tablespoons soy sauce on the duck. Deep-fry for 10 minutes. Mix water, leung leel, salt, sugar, ½ cup soy sauce. Boil duck in this mixture for ½ hour. Remove from pot and cool. Bone. Coat both sides with flour. Deep-fry for 4 minutes on one side and 2 minutes on the other side. Make a gravy by adding cornstarch paste to broth remaining from boiling the duck. Line serving dish with lettuce. Place duck in dish, garnish with almonds and pour gravy over duck.

ROAST DUCK (FOR OPP)

1 fat duck (opp)
1 tablespoon oil
1 tablespoon salt
1 tablespoon minced garlic
1 tablespoon sherry
2 cups and 2 quarts water
2 tablespoons crushed yuen see
(a spice)

1 tablespoon far jeel (a spice)
2 pieces star anise (bok gok)
1 teaspoon monosodium
glutamate
1 teaspoon soy sauce
1 teaspoon sugar
dash of pepper
1 scallion

2 tablespoons honey

Cut a ¼″ hole in the neck of the duck and pump air into this hole with a bicycle pump until the duck is fully blown up. Let air out. Clean the inside of the duck. Place oil and salt in a very hot frying pan. Stir-fry garlic for ½ minute. Sprinkle in sherry. Add yuen see, far jeel, star anise, monosodium glutamate, soy sauce, sugar, pepper and 2 cups water. Simmer for 15 minutes. Strain out far jeel and keep the gravy. Cut scallion into 1-inch pieces and stuff into the duck and pour gravy into the duck from the end. Seal the end with a wire and then tie with a thread so that the gravy will not leak out. Pump up the duck again and tie it up at the neck so that the air will not leak out. Dissolve honey in 2 quarts of water. Pour over duck several times to make the skin crisp. Hang duck up until it dries. Place on rack in roasting pan. Roast for 20 minutes in 450° F. oven. Turn duck over, reduce heat to 300° F. and roast another 10 minutes.

NOTE: You may substitute five-flavored powder (ng heung fun) in place of far jeel, yuen see and bok gok.

Meat

Chinese meat dishes generally are not pure meat dishes such as the American steak, chops, or roasts. The meat is only used in small quantity with an abundance of vegetables to stretch the taste of the meat to its fullest capacity. The proportion of meat to vegetables very often follows Confucius' golden mean of one-fourth meat to three-fourths vegetables.

When the Chinese refer to meat, they are usually referring to pork rather than beef. The ox is a great friend of the farmer in his work on the farm and because of the great help of these animals in the production of rice there is a superstition among some Chinese that it is good luck and blessful not to eat beef. It was morally wrong in some villages to kill an aged ox after his long, faithful service on the paddy field. As a matter of fact many Chinese living in central China have never tasted beef. It is said that the Chinese take better care of their cattle than of themselves. If a draft animal is used for turning the irrigation wheel, the Chinese build a shed to protect the beast from the sun, but if manpower is used, no shelter of any sort is considered necessary. Cattle sheds made of straw and clay are built to house cattle and pigs in Kiangsi.

There is an economic reason why beef is not as plentiful as pork. Most families cannot afford to keep more than one ox because it eats so much and arable land is too scarce to be used for a pasture. The lack of refrigeration also requires that meat processing be done on a small scale. A farmer who slaughters a cow must dispose of it quickly before it spoils either by consuming it, selling it, or drying the meat. As contrasted to the lack of beef dishes in China, Chinese restaurants in America have been influenced by the abundance of beef in this country so that a menu will have as many beef as pork or seafood dishes. Steak Kow, broiled steak with Chinese cabbage and bamboo shoots, is a Chinese adaptation of a popular American cut of meat which comes directly from the American influence.

The favorite meat of the Chinese is pork. Not only are pigs much less expensive to raise than cows but they are lazy animals and the farmer does not feel guilty about slaughtering them as opposed to the ox. Pigs are a token of prosperity and plenty, and roast pig is most commonly used for festive occasions as, for instance, on the occasion of a wedding when the groom's family sends a whole roast pig to the bride's family as a gift.

In Chinese-American restaurants pork is not a very popular item except for roast pork and spare ribs. Steamed pork hash (Jing yook beeng), a favorite at most Chinese homes, is almost never seen at Chinese-American restaurants. Chinese vegetables stir-fried with fresh pork are also not as popular as the same combination with beef. Besides roasting, stir-frying, and steaming pork the Chinese like to use pork to make soups.

CHOPPED BEEF WITH VEGETABLES (NGOW YOOK SOONG)

½ pound chopped beef (ngow yook)
¼ cup Chinese mushrooms (dung goo)
1 cup Chinese celery cabbage (bok choy)
¼ cup peas
¼ cup snow pea pods
½ teaspoon salt or to taste
1 clove crushed garlic
¼ cup diced water chestnuts
¼ cup sliced bamboo shoots
¼ cup water
½ teaspoon monosodium glutamate
½ teaspoon sugar
dash of pepper
1 teaspoon cornstarch mixed with 2 tablespoons water
¼ cup cellophane noodles (fun see)
1 tablespoon crushed almonds

Soak mushrooms in cold water ½ hour to soften. Drain. Mince celery cabbage, mushrooms, snow pea pods (soong). Using a high flame, heat a well-greased frying pan and add salt and garlic. Stir-fry beef for 1 minute. Add mushrooms, celery cabbage, peas, snow pea pods, water chestnuts, bamboo shoots and water. Cover and cook for 3 minutes. Add monosodium glutamate, sugar and pepper. Stir in cornstarch paste. Throw cellophane noodles into a deep fryer of boiling oil. Take out immediately. Garnish dish with crushed almonds and cellophane noodles.

This recipe with sliced beef is the non-Chinese dish chop suey.

BEEF WITH SNOW PEAS (SOOT DOW NGOW)

¼ pound flank steak (ngow)
¼ pound snow pea pods (soot dow)
dash of pepper
½ teaspoon sugar
¼ teaspoon monosodium glutamate
¼ cup water
1 teaspoon soy sauce
1 slice ginger root
¼ teaspoon salt or to taste
1 teaspoon sherry
1 teaspoon cornstarch mixed with 3 tablespoons water

Slice flank steak across the grain into thin slices. String snow peas, leaving the pods intact. Mix pepper, sugar, monosodium glutamate, soy sauce and water. Using a high flame, heat a well-greased frying pan. Add ginger root and salt. Stir-fry the steak for 1 minute, at the same time sprinkling sherry over the meat. Add water mixture and snow pea pods. Cover and cook for 2 minutes. Add the cornstarch paste and cook and stir for ½ minute.

BEEF WITH CURRY (GAR LAY NGOW)

½ pound flank steak (ngow)
1 medium size onion
4 tablespoons curry powder
  (gar lay)
½ cup water
¼ teaspoon salt

1 teaspoon cornstarch mixed
  with 3 tablespoons water
½ teaspoon sugar
½ teaspoon monosodium
  glutamate
dash of pepper

Slice steak across the grain thinly. Slice onion into half rings. Using medium high flame, heat a frying pan without oil. Add onion and stir-fry for 2 minutes. Add curry powder and cook for 5 minutes. Add steak and stir-fry for 2 minutes. Add water and salt and bring stove up to a high flame. Cook for 2 minutes or until it boils. Stir in cornstarch paste, sugar, monosodium glutamate and pepper.

NOTE: This is a dry frying pan, and curry could be reduced according to taste.

BEEF WITH PEAS (CHANG DOW NGOW)

¼ pound flank steak (ngow)
dash of pepper
1 teaspoon soy sauce
¼ teaspoon salt or to taste
¼ teaspoon monosodium
  glutamate

¼ cup water
1 cup peas (chang dow)
1 teaspoon sherry
1 teaspoon cornstarch mixed
  with 3 tablespoons water

Dice flank steak finely. Mix pepper, soy sauce, salt, mono-sodium glutamate and water. Using a high flame, heat a well-greased frying pan. Add peas and stir-fry for ½ minute. Cover and cook for 1 minute. Remove and set aside. Heat and grease the pan again and stir-fry steak for 1 minute, at the same time sprinkling sherry on the meat. Add peas and water mixture. Stir-fry for 2 minutes. Add cornstarch paste and cook and stir for ½ minute.

BEEF WITH CHINESE CABBAGE (BOK CHOY NGOW)

½ pound Chinese celery cabbage (bok choy)
¼ pound flank steak (ngow)
dash of pepper
1 teaspoon soy sauce
¼ teaspoon monosodium glutamate

¼ cup water
¼ teaspoon salt
1 thin slice ginger root
1 teaspoon sherry
1 teaspoon cornstarch mixed with 3 tablespoons water

Slice celery cabbage diagonally. Slice steak across the grain into thin slices. Mix pepper, soy sauce, monosodium gluta-mate and water. Using a high flame, heat a well-greased fry-ing pan and add salt and ginger root. Add celery cabbage and stir-fry for ½ minute. Add water mixture. Cover and cook for 1 minute. Remove and set aside. Heat and grease the pan again and stir-fry steak for 1 minute, at the same time sprinkling sherry over the meat. Add celery cabbage and stir-fry for 2 minutes. Add cornstarch paste and cook and stir for ½ minute.

For Beef With Green Cabbage (Guy Choy Ngow), substitute green cabbage for Chinese celery cabbage.

For Beef With Bitter Melon (Fooh Quar Ngow), substitute ½ pound bitter melon for Chinese celery cabbage. Remove spongy pulp and seeds from inside. Slice into semicircles

¼" thick and follow same directions. Many Americans do not like this dish.

BEEF WITH PICKLED CABBAGE (SHUEN CHOY NGOW)

½ pound pickled cabbage
  (shuen choy)
¼ pound flank steak (ngow)
dash of pepper
1 teaspoon soy sauce
¼ teaspoon monosodium
  glutamate

¼ cup water
¼ teaspoon salt
1 thin slice ginger root
1 teaspoon sherry
1 teaspoon cornstarch mixed
  with 3 tablespoons water

Slice cabbage diagonally. Slice steak across the grain into thin slices. Mix pepper, soy sauce, monosodium glutamate, water, salt and ginger root. Heat a frying pan medium hot without oil. Simmer cabbage in water mixture for 5 minutes. Remove and set aside. Heat and grease the pan and stir-fry steak for 1 minute, at the same time sprinkling sherry over the meat. Add cabbage and stir-fry for 2 minutes. Add cornstarch paste and cook and stir for ½ minute.

BEEF WITH BROCCOLI (GUY LON NGOW)

½ pound broccoli (guy lon)
¼ pound flank steak (ngow)
dash of pepper
1 teaspoon soy sauce
¼ teaspoon salt
¼ teaspoon monosodium
  glutamate

¼ cup water
slice of ginger root
1 teaspoon sherry
1 teaspoon cornstarch mixed
  with 3 tablespoons water

Slice broccoli diagonally. Boil for 4 minutes. Wash in cold water and drain. Slice flank steak across the grain into thin slices. Mix pepper, soy sauce, salt, monosodium glutamate and water. Using a high flame, heat a well-greased frying pan and add ginger. Stir-fry broccoli for ½ minute. Cover and cook for 1 minute. Remove and set aside. Heat and grease the pan again and stir-fry steak for 1 minute, at the same time sprinkling sherry on the meat. Add the broccoli and water mixture and stir. Cover and cook for 2 minutes. Add cornstarch paste and cook and stir for ½ minute.

NOTE: Substitute cauliflower for broccoli. This dish is cooked in Chinese-American homes but not served in Chinese restaurants.

BEEF WITH OYSTER SAUCE (HO YOW NGOW)

¼ pound flank steak (ngow)
1 tablespoon oyster sauce
 (ho yow)
dash of pepper
½ teaspoon sugar
¼ teaspoon monosodium
 glutamate

½ cup water
1 slice of ginger root
1 teaspoon sherry
1½ teaspoons cornstarch
 mixed with 3 tablespoons
 water

Slice steak across the grain into thin slices. Mix oyster sauce, pepper, sugar, monosodium glutamate and water. Using a high flame, heat a well-greased frying pan and add ginger root. Stir-fry for 1 minute, at the same time sprinkling sherry over the meat. Add water mixture. Cook and stir until it comes to a boil. Add cornstarch paste and cook and stir for ½ minute.

BEEF WITH BEAN CURDS (DOW FOO NGOW)

¼ pound flank steak (ngow)
2 bean curds (dow foo)
dash of pepper
1 tablespoon oyster sauce
½ teaspoon soy sauce
½ teaspoon sugar
¼ teaspoon salt

¼ teaspoon monosodium
 glutamate
¾ cup water
1 slice ginger root
1 teaspoon sherry
1½ teaspoon cornstarch mixed
 with 3 tablespoons water

Slice flank steak across the grain into thin slices. Cut each bean curd into 6 pieces. Mix pepper, oyster sauce, soy sauce, sugar, salt, monosodium glutamate and water. Using a high flame, heat a well-greased frying pan and add ginger root. Stir-fry steak for 1 minute, at the same time sprinkling sherry over the meat. Add bean curds and water mixture. Cook and stir until it comes to a boil. Add cornstarch paste and cook and stir for ½ minute.

BEEF WITH GREEN PEPPER, TOMATOES AND ONIONS
(FON CARE LOT TZU NGOW)

¼ pound flank steak (ngow)	½ teaspoon sugar
3 large tomatoes (fon care)	¾ cup water
2 large green peppers (lot tzu)	1 slice ginger root
1 teaspoon black beans (dow see)	1 clove crushed garlic
dash of pepper	1 cup sliced onions
1 teaspoon soy sauce	1 teaspoon sherry
½ teaspoon salt	1½ teaspoons cornstarch mixed with 3 tablespoons water
¼ teaspoon monosodium glutamate	

Slice flank steak across the grain into thin slices. Cut each tomato into 6 pieces and the peppers into 1-inch squares. Wash black beans. Mix pepper, soy sauce, salt, monosodium glutamate, sugar and water. Using a high flame, heat a well-greased frying pan and add ginger, black beans, garlic, green peppers and onions and stir-fry for 1 minute. Add water mixture and cover and cook for 3 minutes. Remove and set aside. Heat and grease the frying pan again and add ginger root. Stir-fry steak for 1 minute, at the same time sprinkling sherry over the meat. Add green peppers and onions. When it comes to a boil, add tomatoes and cornstarch paste and cook and stir for ½ minute.

BEEF WITH STRING BEANS (DOW JAI NGOW)

¼ pound flank steak (ngow)
¼ pound string beans
   (dow jai)
dash of pepper
1 teaspoon soy sauce
¼ teaspoon salt or to taste
¼ teaspoon monosodium
   glutamate

¼ cup water
1 clove garlic
2 teaspoons brown bean sauce
   (mien see) optional
1 thin slice ginger root
1 teaspoon sherry
1 teaspoon cornstarch mixed
   with 3 tablespoons water

Slice the flank steak across the grain into thin slices. Boil string beans 4 minutes. Wash in cold water and drain. Mix pepper, soy sauce, salt, monosodium glutamate and water. Using a high flame, heat a well-greased frying pan and add garlic. Add brown bean sauce and string beans and stir-fry for 1 minute. Remove and set aside. Heat and grease the pan again and add ginger root. Stir-fry the beef for 1 minute, at the same time sprinkling sherry over the meat. Add the string beans and cornstarch paste and cook and stir for ½ minute.

BEEF WITH BEAN SPROUTS (NGAR CHOY NGOW)

¼ pound flank steak (ngow)
½ pound bean sprouts
   (ngar choy)
dash of pepper
1 teaspoon soy sauce
¼ teaspoon monosodium
   glutamate

¼ teaspoon sugar
3 tablespoons water
¼ teaspoon salt or to taste
1 slice ginger root
1 teaspoon sherry
1 teaspoon cornstarch mixed
   with 3 tablespoons water

Slice steak across the grain into thin slices. Wash bean sprouts and drain. Mix pepper, soy sauce, monosodium glutamate, sugar and water. Using a high flame, heat a well-greased frying pan and add salt. Add bean sprouts and stir-fry for ½ minute. Cover and cook for 1 minute. Remove and set aside.

Heat and grease the pan again and add ginger root. Stir-fry steak for 1 minute, at the same time sprinkling sherry on the meat. Add bean sprouts and the water mixture and stir. Cover and cook for 2 minutes. Add cornstarch paste and cook and stir for ½ minute.

BEEF WITH ONIONS (CHUNG TOW NGOW)

¼ pound flank steak (ngow)
2 large onions (chung tow)
dash of pepper
1 teaspoon soy sauce
¼ teaspoon salt
¼ teaspoon monosodium glutamate
½ teaspoon sugar

¾ cup water
2 tablespoons oil
1 clove crushed garlic
1 slice ginger root
1 teaspoon sherry
1½ teaspoons cornstarch mixed with 3 tablespoons water

Slice flank steak across the grain into thin slices. Slice onions into half rings. Mix pepper, soy sauce, salt, monosodium glutamate, sugar and water. Using a high flame, heat a well-greased frying pan and add 1 tablespoon oil and garlic. Stir-fry onions for 1 minute. Add water mixture, cover and cook for 3 minutes. Remove and set aside. Heat the frying pan again and add 1 tablespoon oil and ginger root. Add steak and stir-fry for 1 minute, at the same time sprinkling sherry over the meat. Add the onions. When it comes to a boil, mix in the cornstarch paste and cook and stir for ½ minute.

BEEF WITH TOMATOES (FON CARE NGOW)

¼ pound flank steak (ngow)
3 large tomatoes (fon care)
dash of pepper
1 teaspoon soy sauce
¼ teaspoon salt
¼ teaspoon monosodium glutamate

½ teaspoon sugar
½ cup water
1 slice ginger root
1 teaspoon sherry
1½ teaspoons cornstarch mixed with 3 tablespoons water

Slice the flank steak across the grain into thin slices. Cut each tomato into 6 pieces. Mix pepper, soy sauce, salt, monosodium glutamate, sugar and water. Using a high flame, heat a well-greased frying pan and add ginger root. Add steak and stir-fry for 1 minute, at the same time sprinkling sherry over the meat. Add tomatoes and water mixture and cook and stir until it boils. Mix in the cornstarch paste and cook and stir for 1/2 minute.

BEEF WITH MUSHROOMS (MOO GOO NGOW)

1/4 pound flank steak (ngow)
dash of pepper
1 teaspoon soy sauce
1/4 teaspoon salt or to taste
1/4 teaspoon monosodium
  glutamate
1/2 teaspoon sugar
3/4 cup water

1 slice ginger root
1 teaspoon sherry
1/4 cup sliced canned
  mushrooms (moo goo)
1 1/2 teaspoons cornstarch
  mixed with 3 tablespoons
  water

Slice the flank steak across the grain into thin slices. Mix pepper, soy sauce, salt, monosodium glutamate, sugar and water. Using a high flame, heat a well-greased frying pan and add ginger root. Add steak and stir-fry for 1 minute, at the same time sprinkling sherry over the meat. Add mushrooms and water mixture. Cook and stir until it comes to a boil. Add cornstarch paste and cook and stir for 1/2 minute.

BEEF WITH CELLOPHANE NOODLES (FUN SEE NGOW)

Fun see is often called cellophane noodles or long rice and can be bought at Chinese groceries in fried form. They will soak up a lot of water when cooking and may require more water than the recipe calls for.

¼ pound cellophane noodles
   (fun see)
1 cup Chinese celery cabbage
   (bok choy)
¼ cup Chinese mushrooms
   (dung goo)
¼ pound flank steak (ngow)

4 tablespoons oil
½ teaspoon salt
1 quart water
½ teaspoon sugar
½ teaspoon soy sauce
1 teaspoon monosodium
   glutamate

dash of pepper

Soak cellophane noodles and mushrooms for ½ hour in cold water to soften. Drain. Shred steak, celery cabbage and mushrooms into pieces of 1½″ x ⅛″ x ⅛″. Into a very hot deep frying pan place 2 tablespoons oil and salt. Stir-fry the steak for 2 minutes. Add water, sugar, soy sauce, monosodium glutamate, pepper, noodles, celery cabbage and mushrooms. Bring to a boil and simmer for 5 minutes. Add 2 tablespoons oil and cook and stir for 2 minutes.

The banquet version of this recipe is described on p. 76.

STEAMED BEEF WITH SALTED CABBAGE
(CHUNG CHOY JING NGOW YOOK)

1 pound flank steak
   (ngow yook)
1 cup salted cabbage
   (chung choy)
½ teaspoon cornstarch
½ teaspoon sugar
½ teaspoon soy sauce

¼ teaspoon salt or to taste
½ teaspoon monosodium
   glutamate
dash of pepper
2 teaspoons oil
2 tablespoons water

Slice flank steak across the grain into thin slices. Slice cabbage thinly. Mix meat, cornstarch, sugar, soy sauce, salt, monosodium glutamate, pepper and 1 teaspoon oil. Add water and cabbage. Place in shallow dish and cover. Steam for 15 minutes (jing). Add 1 tablespoon oil on top before serving.

See Guide to Chinese Ingredients for salted cabbage.

STEAMED GROUND PORK WITH SALTED EGG
(HOM DON JING GEE YOK)

This is very popular in Chinese homes but seldom served in restaurants.

1 salted egg (hom don)
1 pound ground pork (gee yok)
2 water chestnuts
1 teaspoon cornstarch
½ teaspoon monosodium glutamate
½ teaspoon salt
½ teaspoon sugar
4 tablespoons water
dash of pepper
½ teaspoon soy sauce
1 tablespoon oil

Chop water chestnuts finely. Mix all ingredients with the egg white. Mash the egg yolk and place on top of mixture. Steam for 15 minutes (jing).

See Guide to Chinese Ingredients for salted egg.

BARBECUE SPARE RIBS (SHEW PAI QUOT)

1½ pounds spare ribs (pai quot)
2 tablespoons soy sauce
4 tablespoons salt
4 tablespoons sugar
4 cloves crushed garlic
3 tablespoons haisein sauce
¼ cup hot water

Mix soy sauce, salt, sugar, garlic, haisein sauce and water. Marinate the spare ribs for ½ hour. Place on rack in baking pan. Bake at 375° F. for 15 minutes, turn ribs over (shew). Reduce heat to 250° F. and bake 10 minutes more.

NOTE: Served with duck sauce (see Guide to Chinese Ingredients).

DEEP-FRIED SPARE RIBS WITH GRAVY (SO JAR PAI QUOT)

½ pound spare ribs (pai quot)
1½ teaspoons soy sauce
¼ teaspoon salt
2¼ teaspoons sugar
1 teaspoon sherry
2 teaspoons cornstarch
1 clove crushed garlic

¼ cup water
1 tablespoon vinegar
½ teaspoon monosodium
  glutamate
1 teaspoon cornstarch mixed
  with 3 tablespoons water
dash of pepper

Cut spare ribs into 1-inch pieces. Mix 1 teaspoon soy sauce, ¼ teaspoon salt, ¼ teaspoon sugar and 1 teaspoon sherry. Marinate spare ribs for 5 minutes. Coat with cornstarch, and deep-fry. Spare ribs will float when done. Using a high flame, heat a well-greased frying pan and add garlic. Add ¼ cup water, 1 tablespoon vinegar, 2 teaspoons sugar, ½ teaspoon soy sauce and ½ teaspoon monosodium glutamate. Bring to a boil. Stir in cornstarch paste and dash of pepper. Pour gravy over spare ribs and stir.

ROAST PORK (CHAR SHU)

Pork cooked in this way is used in many recipes which follow. Make some extra char shu so that you can try these recipes.

1 pound pork tenderloin
½ cup water
1 tablespoon salt

4 tablespoons sugar
¼ cup soy sauce
½ teaspoon tomato coloring

Heat water and dissolve salt and sugar. Add soy sauce and tomato coloring. Marinate the pork for at least ½ hour. Place on rack in baking pan. Bake at 375° F. for 15 minutes, turn pork over. Reduce heat to 250° F. and bake 10 minutes more.

NOTE: Served with duck sauce (see Guide to Chinese Ingredients).

ROAST PORK WITH BEAN SPROUTS
(CHAR SHU NGAR CHOY)

¼ pound roast pork
(char shu)
½ pound bean sprouts (ngar choy)
dash of pepper
1 teaspoon soy sauce
¼ teaspoon monosodium glutamate

¼ teaspoon sugar
3 tablespoons water
¼ teaspoon salt or to taste
1 teaspoon cornstarch mixed with 3 tablespoons water

Shred roast pork across the grain into pieces of 1½" x ⅛" x ⅛". Wash bean sprouts and drain. Mix pepper, soy sauce, monosodium glutamate, sugar and water. Using a high flame, heat well-greased frying pan and add salt. Stir-fry bean sprouts for ½ minute. Cover and cook for 1 minute. Remove and set aside. Heat and grease the pan again. Stir-fry roast pork for 1 minute. Add bean sprouts and water mixture. Cover and cook for 2 minutes. Add cornstarch paste and cook and stir for ½ minute.

ROAST PORK WITH CHINESE CELERY CABBAGE
(BOK CHOY CHAR SHU)

¼ pound roast pork
(char shu), p. 142
½ pound Chinese celery cabbage (bok choy)
dash of pepper
1 teaspoon soy sauce
¼ teaspoon monosodium glutamate

¼ cup water
¼ teaspoon salt or to taste
1 thin slice ginger root
1 teaspoon cornstarch mixed with 3 tablespoons water

Slice roast pork across the grain into thin slices. Slice celery cabbage diagonally. Mix pepper, soy sauce, monosodium glutamate and water. Using a high flame, heat a well-greased frying pan and add salt and ginger root. Add celery cabbage. Stir-fry for ½ minute. Cover and cook for 1 minute. Remove and set aside. Heat and grease the pan again and stir-fry roast pork for 1 minute. Add celery cabbage and water mixture. Cover and cook for 2 minutes. Add cornstarch paste and cook and stir for ½ minute.

ROAST PORK WITH MUSHROOMS (MOO GOO CHAR SHU)

¼ pound roast pork (char shu), p. 142
dash of pepper
1 teaspoon soy sauce
½ teaspoon sugar
¼ teaspoon monosodium glutamate

¾ cup water
¼ teaspoon salt
½ cup sliced canned mushrooms (moo goo)
1½ teaspoon cornstarch mixed with 3 tablespoons water

Slice roast pork across the grain into thin slices. Mix pepper, soy sauce, sugar, monosodium glutamate and water. Using a high flame, heat a well-greased frying pan and add salt. Stir-fry the roast pork for 1 minute. Add mushrooms and water mixture. Stir until it comes to a boil. Add the cornstarch paste and cook and stir for ½ minute.

ROAST PORK WITH CHINESE SNOW PEAS (SOOT DOW CHAR SHU)

¼ pound snow pea pods (soot dow)
¼ pound roast pork (char shu), p. 142
dash of pepper
¼ teaspoon salt or to taste
½ teaspoon sugar

¼ teaspoon monosodium glutamate
1 teaspoon soy sauce
3 tablespoons water
1 teaspoon cornstarch mixed with 3 tablespoons water

Slice roast pork across the grain into thin slices. String the snow peas leaving the pods intact and wash. Mix pepper,

salt, sugar, monosodium glutamate, soy sauce and water.
Using a high flame, heat a well-greased frying pan. Stir-fry
snow pea pods for 1/2 minute. Cover and cook for 1 minute.
Remove and set aside. Heat and grease the pan again. Stir-fry
roast pork for 1 minute. Add snow pea pods and stir. Add
water mixture. Cover and cook for 2 minutes. Add cornstarch paste and cook and stir for 1/2 minute.

ROAST PORK WITH BEAN CURDS (DOW FOO CHAR SHU)

1/2 pound roast pork
  (char shu), p. 142
2 bean curds (dow foo)
dash of pepper
1 tablespoon oyster sauce
1/2 teaspoon soy sauce
1/2 teaspoon sugar

1/4 teaspoon salt
1/4 teaspoon monosodium
  glutamate
3/4 cup water
1 1/2 teaspoons cornstarch
  mixed with 3 tablespoons
  water

Slice roast pork across the grain into thin slices. Cut each
bean curd into 6 pieces. Mix pepper, oyster sauce, soy sauce,
sugar, salt, monosodium glutamate with water. Using a high
flame, heat a well-greased frying pan. Stir-fry roast pork for 1
minute. Add bean curds and water mixture. Cook and stir
until it comes to a boil. Add cornstarch paste and cook and
stir for 1/2 minute.

PORK WITH BEAN SPROUTS (NGAR CHOY GEE YOK)

1/4 pound pork (gee yok)
1/2 pound bean sprouts
  (ngar choy)
dash of pepper
1 teaspoon soy sauce
1/4 teaspoon sugar
1/4 teaspoon monosodium
  glutamate

3 tablespoons water
1/4 teaspoon salt or to taste
1 teaspoon sherry
1 teaspoon cornstarch mixed
  with 3 tablespoons water

Shred pork across the grain into pieces of 1½" x ⅛" x ⅛".
Wash bean sprouts and drain. Mix pepper, soy sauce, sugar,
monosodium glutamate and water. Using a high flame, heat
a well-greased frying pan and add salt. Add bean sprouts and
stir-fry for ½ minute. Cover and cook for 1 minute. Remove
and set aside. Heat and grease the pan again. Stir-fry pork
for 2 minutes, at the same time sprinkling sherry over the
meat. Add bean sprouts and water mixture. Cover and cook
for 2 minutes. Add cornstarch paste and cook and stir for
½ minute.

DICED ROAST PORK WITH CHINESE VEGETABLES
(CHAR SHU DING)

½ pound roast pork (char shu), p. 142	¼ cup celery
¼ cup almonds	¼ teaspoon salt
½ cup mushrooms	¼ cup water
½ pound Chinese celery cabbage (bok choy)	1 teaspoon cornstarch mixed with 3 tablespoons water
4 water chestnuts	dash of pepper
¼ cup bamboo shoots	¼ teaspoon sugar
12 snow pea pods	½ teaspoon monosodium glutamate

Deep-fry almonds for 3 minutes. Allow to cool. Dice roast
pork, mushrooms, celery cabbage, water chestnuts, bamboo
shoots, snow pea pods and celery into ¼" cubes (ding).
Using a high flame, heat a well-greased frying pan and add
salt. Add mushrooms, celery cabbage, water chestnuts, bamboo shoots, snow pea pods and celery. Stir-fry for ½ minute.
Add water. Cover and cook for 2 minutes. Add roast pork
and stir. Add cornstarch paste, pepper, sugar, monosodium
glutamate and cook and stir for ½ minute. Place in serving
dish and garnish with almonds.

PORK WITH TOMATOES, GREEN PEPPERS AND ONIONS
(FON CARE LOT TZU GEE)

¼ pound pork (gee yok)
3 large tomatoes (fon care)
2 large green peppers (lot tzu)
1 teaspoon black beans
    (dow see)
1 large onion
dash of pepper
1 teaspoon soy sauce
½ teaspoon salt

¼ teaspoon monosodium
    glutamate
½ teaspoon sugar
¾ cup water
1 clove crushed garlic
1 teaspoon sherry
1½ teaspoons cornstarch
    mixed with 3 tablespoons
    water

Slice pork across the grain into thin slices. Cut each tomato into 6 pieces and peppers into 1-inch squares. Mash black beans. Slice onion into half rings. Mix pepper, soy sauce, salt, monosodium glutamate, sugar and water. Using a high flame, heat a well-greased frying pan and add garlic and black beans. Add green peppers and onion and stir-fry for 1 minute. Add water mixture. Cover and cook for 3 minutes. Remove and set aside. Heat and grease the pan again. Stir-fry pork for 2 minutes, at the same time sprinkling sherry over the meat. Add green peppers, onion, tomatoes and corn-starch paste and cook and stir for ½ minute.

PORK WITH CHINESE CABBAGE
(BOK CHOY CHOW GEE YOK)

¼ pound pork (gee yok)
½ pound Chinese celery
    cabbage (bok choy)
dash of pepper
1 teaspoon soy sauce
¼ teaspoon monosodium
    glutamate

¼ cup water
¼ teaspoon salt or to taste
1 teaspoon sherry
1 teaspoon cornstarch mixed
    with 3 tablespoons water

Slice pork across the grain into thin slices. Slice celery cabbage diagonally. Mix pepper, soy sauce, monosodium glutamate and water. Using a high flame, heat a well-greased frying pan and add salt. Add celery cabbage and stir-fry for ½ minute. Cover and cook for 1 minute. Remove and set aside. Heat and grease the pan again and stir-fry (chow) pork for 2 minutes, at the same time sprinkling sherry over the meat. Add celery cabbage and water mixture. Cover and cook for 2 minutes. Add cornstarch paste and cook and stir for ½ minute.

For Pork With Bitter Melon (Fooh Quar Gee Yok), substitute ½ pound fooh quar (bitter melon) for celery cabbage. Remove spongy pulp and seeds from inside. Slice into semi-circles ¼" thick and follow same directions. Many Americans do not like this dish.

PORK WITH ONIONS (CHUNG TOW GEE YOK)

¼ pound pork (gee yok)	¾ cup water
2 large onions (chung tow)	1 clove crushed garlic
dash of pepper	¼ teaspoon salt or to taste
1 teaspoon soy sauce	1 teaspoon sherry
¼ teaspoon monosodium glutamate	1½ teaspoons cornstarch mixed with 3 tablespoons water
½ teaspoon sugar	

Slice pork across the grain into thin slices. Slice onions into half rings. Mix pepper, soy sauce, monosodium glutamate, sugar and water. Using a high flame, heat a well-greased frying pan and add garlic. Add onions and stir-fry for 1 minute. Add ¼ cup of water mixture. Cover and cook for 3 minutes. Remove and set aside. Heat and grease pan again and add salt. Stir-fry pork for 2 minutes, at the same time sprinkling sherry over the meat. Add onions and remaining ½ cup of water mixture. When it comes to a boil, add cornstarch paste and cook and stir for ½ minute.

PORK WITH MUSHROOMS (MOO GOO GEE YOK)

¼ pound pork (gee yok)
dash of pepper
1 teaspoon soy sauce
¼ teaspoon salt or to taste
¼ teaspoon monosodium
  glutamate
½ teaspoon sugar

¾ cup water
1 teaspoon sherry
½ cup sliced canned
  mushrooms (moo goo)
1½ teaspoons cornstarch
  mixed with 3 tablespoons
  water

Slice pork across the grain into thin slices. Mix pepper, soy sauce, salt, monosodium glutamate, sugar and water. Using a high flame, heat a well-greased frying pan. Stir-fry pork for 2 minutes, at the same time sprinkling sherry over the meat. Add mushrooms and water mixture. Cook until it comes to a boil. Add cornstarch paste and cook and stir for ½ minute.

For Pork With Tomatoes (Fon Care Gee Yok) reduce water to ½ cup and substitute 3 large tomatoes cut into 6 pieces each for mushrooms.

PORK WITH BROCCOLI (GUY LON GEE YOK)

¼ pound pork (gee yok)
½ pound broccoli (guy lon)
dash of pepper
1 teaspoon soy sauce
¼ teaspoon monosodium
  glutamate

¼ cup water
¼ teaspoon salt or to taste
1 teaspoon sherry
1 teaspoon cornstarch mixed
  with 3 tablespoons water

Slice pork across the grain into thin slices. Slice broccoli diagonally. Boil broccoli for 4 minutes. Wash in cold water and drain. Mix pepper, soy sauce, monosodium glutamate and water. Using a hig flame, heat a well-greased frying pan and add salt. Stir-fry broccoli for ½ minute. Remove and set aside. Heat and grease pan again and stir-fry pork for 2 minutes, at the same time sprinkling sherry over the meat. Add broccoli and water mixture and stir. Cover and cook for 2 minutes. Add cornstarch paste and cook and stir for ½ minute.

PORK WITH PEAS (CHANG DOW GEE YOK)

¼ pound pork (gee yok)	¼ teaspoon salt or to taste
dash of pepper	2 cups peas (chang dow)
1 teaspoon soy sauce	1 teaspoon sherry
¼ teaspoon monosodium glutamate	1 teaspoon cornstarch mixed with 3 tablespoons water
¼ cup water	

Dice pork finely. Mix pepper, soy sauce, monosodium glutamate and water. Using a high flame, heat a well-greased frying pan and add salt. Stir-fry peas for ½ minute. Cover and cook for 1 minute. Remove and set aside. Heat and grease pan again and stir-fry pork for 2 minutes, at the same time sprinkling sherry over the meat. Add peas and water mixture. Cover and cook for 2 minutes. Add cornstarch paste and cook and stir for ½ minute.

PORK WITH SNOW PEAS (SOOT DOW CHOW GEE YOK)

¼ pound pork (gee yok)	1 teaspoon cornstarch mixed with 3 tablespoons water
¼ pound snow pea pods (soot dow)	1 teaspoon soy sauce
¼ teaspoon salt or to taste	½ teaspoon sugar
1 teaspoon sherry	¼ teaspoon monosodium glutamate
¼ cup water	
dash of pepper	

Slice pork across the grain into thin slices. String snow peas, keeping the pods intact. Using a high flame, heat a well-greased frying pan and add salt. Stir-fry (chow) pork for 2 minutes, at the same time sprinkling sherry over the meat. Add snow pea pods and water. Cover and cook for 2 minutes. Add cornstarch paste, soy sauce, sugar, monosodium glutamate and pepper. Stir.

PORK WITH OYSTER SAUCE (HO YOW GEE YOK)

¼ pound pork (gee yok)
1 tablespoon oyster sauce (ho yow)
dash of pepper
½ teaspoon sugar
¼ teaspoon monosodium glutamate

½ cup water
1 teaspoon sherry
1½ teaspoons cornstarch mixed with 3 tablespoons water

Slice pork across the grain into thin slices. Mix oyster sauce, pepper, sugar, monosodium glutamate and water. Using a high flame, heat a well-greased frying pan. Stir-fry pork for 2 minutes, at the same time sprinkling sherry over the meat. Add water mixture. Cook and stir until it comes to a boil. Add cornstarch paste and cook and stir for ½ minute.

CURRIED PORK (GAR LAY GEE YOK)

½ pound pork (gee yok)
¼ cup sliced onions
4 tablespoons curry powder (gar lay)
½ cup water
¼ teaspoon salt or to taste

1 teaspoon cornstarch mixed with 3 tablespoons water
½ teaspoon monosodium glutamate
½ teaspoon sugar
dash of pepper

Slice pork across the grain into thin pieces. Using a medium flame, heat frying pan without oil. Add onions and stir-fry for 2 minutes. Add curry powder and pork and stir-fry for 5 minutes more. Add water and salt and bring flame to high heat. Cook and stir for 4 minutes. Add cornstarch paste, monosodium glutamate, sugar and pepper. Stir.

NOTE: This is a dry frying pan and curry powder could be reduced according to taste.

PORK WITH CELLOPHANE NOODLES (FUN SEE GEE YOK)

Fun see is often called cellophane noodles or long rice and can be bought at Chinese groceries in dried form. It will soak up a lot of water when cooking and may require more water than the recipe calls for.

¼ pound cellophane noodles (fun see)
¼ cup dried shrimp (har mei)
¼ cup Chinese mushrooms (dung goo)
¼ pound pork (gee yok)
1 cup Chinese celery cabbage (bok choy)

4 tablespoons oil
½ teaspoon salt
1 quart water
½ teaspoon sugar
½ teaspoon soy sauce
1 teaspoon monosodium glutamate
dash of pepper

Soak noodles, dried shrimps, mushrooms for ½ hour in cold water to soften. Drain. Shred pork and celery cabbage into pieces of 1½″ x ⅛″ x ⅛″. Using a high flame, heat a deep frying pan. Add 2 tablespoons oil and salt. Stir-fry the pork for 2 minutes. Add water, sugar, soy sauce, monosodium glutamate, pepper, noodles, celery cabbage, mushrooms and shrimp. Bring to a boil, then reduce heat and simmer for 5 minutes. Add 2 tablespoons oil and cook and stir for 2 minutes.

STEAMED GROUND PORK WITH WATER CHESTNUTS
(MAR TAI YOK BENG)

1 pound ground pork (gee yok)	½ teaspoon salt
	½ teaspoon sugar
6 water chestnuts (mar tai)	4 tablespoons water
1 teaspoon cornstarch	dash of pepper
½ teaspoon monosodium glutamate	½ teaspoon soy sauce
	1 tablespoon oil

Mince water chestnuts (the finer you mince the better the dish will taste). Mix all ingredients. Place in a dish, cover and steam for 15 minutes.

Beng means cake. When steamed the ground pork will look like a flat cake.

FRIED WONTON

¼ pound ground pork	2 minced water chestnuts
¼ teaspoon salt	24 pieces wonton skins
½ teaspoon monosodium glutamate	1 beaten egg

Mix all ingredients. Wrap wontons and seal with egg by following diagram p. 88. Deep-fry in boiling oil for 2 minutes.

STEAMED PORK WITH SALTED CABBAGE
(CHUNG CHOY JING GEE YOK)

1 pound pork (gee yok)	¼ teaspoon salt
1 cup salted cabbage (chung choy)	½ teaspoon monosodium glutamate
½ teaspoon cornstarch	dash of pepper
½ teaspoon sugar	2 teaspoons oil
½ teaspoon soy sauce	2 tablespoons water

Slice pork and salted cabbage into thin slices. Mix pork,

cornstarch, sugar, soy sauce, salt, monosodium glutamate, pepper, and 1 teaspoon oil. Add water and salted cabbage. Place in a dish, cover and steam for 15 minutes (jing). Spread 1 teaspoon oil over top before serving.

For salted cabbage, see Guide to Chinese Ingredients.

STEAMED GROUND PORK WITH HAM
(FOR TUI JING GEE YOK BENG)

1 pound ground pork (gee yok)	½ teaspoon salt
	½ teaspoon sugar
¼ cup Smithfield ham (for tui)	4 tablespoons water
	dash of pepper
2 water chestnuts	½ teaspoon soy sauce
1 teaspoon cornstarch	1 tablespoon oil
½ teaspoon monosodium glutamate	

Mince ham and water chestnuts very finely. Mix all ingredients and place in dish. Cover and steam for 15 minutes (jing).

SWEET AND SOUR PORK CUBES (NIW GOO YOK)

½ pound pork tenderloin	1½ teaspoons soy sauce
3 tablespoons flour	½ teaspoon monosodium glutamate
¼ cup sliced green peppers	
1 ring pineapple	dash of pepper
¼ cup sliced carrots	2 teaspoons cornstarch mixed with 3 tablespoons water
½ teaspoon salt	
1 clove crushed garlic	¼ cup vinegar
5 tablespoons sugar	½ cup water

Cut pork into 1-inch squares. Roll in flour. Deep-fry in boiling oil. Pork will float when done. Boil green peppers for 3 minutes and drain. Slice pineapple in 1-inch pieces. Using a high flame, heat a well-greased frying pan and add salt and garlic. Add water, vinegar, soy sauce, sugar, monosodium glutamate, and pepper. Bring this mixture to a boil. Add cornstarch paste and cook and stir for ½ minute. Add green peppers, carrots, pineapple and pork and cook for ½ minute more.

For Sweet And Sour Spare Ribs (Tiem Shuen Pei Quot), substitute spare ribs for pork tenderloin. Cut ribs into individual inch-long pieces.

STEAMED GROUND PORK WITH CHINESE PORK SAUSAGE
(LOP CHONG YOK BENG)

1 pound ground pork (yok beng)	½ teaspoon salt
2 pork sausages (lop chong)	½ teaspoon sugar
2 water chestnuts	4 tablespoons water
1 teaspoon cornstarch	dash of pepper
½ teaspoon monosodium glutamate	½ teaspoon soy sauce
	1 tablespoon oil

Mince pork sausage and water chestnuts. Mix all ingredients. Place in dish, cover and steam for 15 minutes.

For pork sausage see Guide to Chinese Ingredients.

Vegetables (Quar Choy)

One of the most frequent comments about Chinese food is that the vegetables are always so crisp and green. This is one of the secrets of Chinese cooking. As we have emphasized again and again, vegetables have to be quick-cooked. Most vegetables do not take more than 4 minutes of cooking if you are using a hot pan.

All of the popular Chinese vegetables have been described in Chapter 3. Don't be discouraged if you cannot obtain these items because a basic recipe like Chow Bok Choy (stir-fried Chinese celery cabbage) can be adapted for American vegetables such as broccoli, celery, onions, green peppers, tomatoes, string beans, peas, and cauliflower. The use of Chinese methods for cooking American vegetables will add a new dimension to every American kitchen. The Chinese in America have been doing it for years. Recipes such as Stir-Fried Cauliflower With Pork (Year Choy Chow Gee Yok), Pork With Tomatoes (Fon Care Chow Gee Yok), Beef With Broccoli (Guy Lon Ngow), Beef With String Beans (Dow Jai Ngow), Shrimps With Tomato Sauce (Fon Care Har Look) and many more are found in this book.

CHINESE CELERY CABBAGE (CHOW BOK CHOY)

½ pound Chinese celery cabbage (bok choy)
2 slices ginger root
¼ teaspoon salt or to taste
3 tablespoons water

¼ teaspoon sugar
¼ teaspoon monosodium glutamate
pinch golden needles (gum jum) (optional)
dash of pepper

Slice celery cabbage diagonally. Using a high flame, heat a well-greased frying pan. Add ginger root and salt. Add other ingredients and stir-fry (chow) for ½ minute. Cover and cook for 2 minutes.

COMBINATION CHINESE VEGETABLES (CHOP CHOY)

1 cup bean sprouts
¼ pound Chinese celery cabbage (bok choy)
¼ cup bamboo shoots
4 water chestnuts

12 snow pea pods
¼ teaspoon salt or to taste
¼ teaspoon sugar
¼ teaspoon monosodium glutamate
3 tablespoons water

Wash bean sprouts in several changes of water and drain. Slice celery cabbage diagonally. Slice bamboo shoots and water chestnuts. Using a high flame, heat a well-greased frying pan. Add salt. Add all other ingredients and stir-fry for ½ minute. Cover and cook for 2 minutes.

BEAN SPROUTS (NGAR CHOY)

½ pound bean sprouts
   (ngar choy)
¼ teaspoon salt or to taste
3 tablespoons water

¼ teaspoon sugar
¼ teaspoon monosodium
   glutamate
dash of pepper

Wash bean sprouts in several changes of water and drain. Using a high flame, heat a well-greased frying pan and add salt. Add all other ingredients and stir-fry for ½ minute. Cover and cook for 2 minutes.

For Snow Peas (Chow Soot Dow) substitute 2 dozen snow pea pods (soot dow) for bean sprouts.

For Spinach Cantonese (Chow Bor Choy), substitute 1 pound spinach (bor choy) for bean sprouts.

MUSHROOMS AND GRAVY (MOO GOO WOO)

1 cup sliced canned
   mushrooms (moo goo)
¼ teaspoon salt or to taste
1 teaspoon soy sauce
1 teaspoon sherry
½ teaspoon sugar

¼ teaspoon monosodium
   glutamate
dash of pepper
¾ cup water
2 teaspoons cornstarch mixed
   with 3 tablespoons water

Using a high flame, heat a well-greased frying pan and add salt. Add mushrooms, soy sauce, sherry, sugar, monosodium glutamate, pepper, and water. Bring to a boil. Add cornstarch paste and cook and stir for ½ minute.

For Water Chestnuts And Gravy (Mar Tai), substitute ½ cup sliced water chestnuts for mushrooms.

Woo means gravy.

CHINESE MUSHROOMS (MUN DUNG GOO)

¼ pound Chinese mushrooms (dung goo)
1 clove garlic
1 star anise (bok gok)

2½ cups water
1 cup oil
3 teaspoons sherry
1½ teaspoons sugar

Soak mushrooms for 1 hour in cold water and drain. Using a high flame, heat a well-greased frying pan and add garlic. Add all other ingredients, cover and simmer for 45 minutes (mun).

NOTE: This is a banquet dish, served by itself, and the 1 cup oil is not a typographical error.

STUFFED GREEN PEPPERS (YUNG LOT TZU)

6 green peppers (lot tzu)
1 pound fish fillet
1 teaspoon salt
½ teaspoon pepper
2 cups water
1 tablespoon oil
1 teaspoon sherry

1 teaspoon soy sauce
1 teaspoon monosodium glutamate
½ teaspoon sugar
1½ teaspoons cornstarch mixed with 3 tablespoons water

Cut green peppers in half and clean the inside. Mince fish very finely. Mix ¾ teaspoon salt, pepper and ½ cup water. Add one half of this mixture to fish and stir for 5 minutes. Add the other half and stir for 5 minutes more. The longer you stir the better it is. Add oil and stir. Stuff the green peppers with this mixture (yung). Using a high flame, heat a well-greased frying pan and fry the peppers on the open side until brown. Add 1½ cups water. Cover and cook for 4 minutes. Remove peppers and set aside. Add sherry, soy sauce, monosodium glutamate, sugar, ¼ teaspoon salt and cornstarch paste. Stir and cook for 1 minute. Pour over the peppers.

Eggs

Americans think of eggs mainly as a breakfast food whereas the Chinese think of them as a dinner dish. Eggs, being very versatile, have been the subject of complete cookbooks and in this chapter we hope to add to your collection of egg recipes. Egg foo young is the most famous Chinese egg dish in America. The Chinese have boiled eggs and fried eggs but these are usually dipped or sprinkled with soy sauce. The only time that the Chinese poach eggs is in soup stock as you will see in the recipes for Water Cress Soup or Bean Curd Soup.

EGG FOO YOUNG (BASIC RECIPE)

3 eggs	½ cup diced roast pork (char shu,
½ cup diced onions	p. 142) or Virginia ham

Mix onion and roast pork. Beat eggs and stir into pork and onions. Use high heat through whole procedure. Bring 2½ inches of oil to boil in a frying pan. Pour one third of egg mixture into the pan. Brown for two minutes. Use a ladle and splash the top of the omelet with the boiling oil so that the top will be hardened. Flip the omelet over. Brown for 1½ minutes. Remove and drain. Repeat for the remaining mixture.

GRAVY FOR EGG FOO YOUNG

1 cup water
1 tablespoon oil
1 teaspoon sugar
1 teaspoon salt
1 teaspoon soy sauce

1 teaspoon monosodium glutamate
dash of pepper
1 teaspoon cornstarch mixed with 2 tablespoons water

Bring water to boil and add all ingredients. Stir for ½ minute.

CHICKEN EGG FOO YOUNG

3 eggs
½ cup diced onions
½ cup diced boiled chicken

¼ cup diced canned mushrooms

Mix and cook according to Egg Foo Young Basic Recipe directions, p. 160.

SUBGUM EGG FOO YOUNG

3 eggs
¼ cup diced onions
½ cup diced roast pork (char shu)

¼ cup diced green pepper
¼ cup diced canned mushrooms

Mix and cook according to Egg Foo Young Basic Recipe directions, p. 160.

SHRIMP EGG FOO YOUNG

3 eggs   1 cup diced onions
½ cup diced boiled shrimp   ½ cup bean sprouts

Mix and cook according to Egg Foo Young Basic Recipe directions, p. 160.

DEEP-FRIED EGGS WITH VEGETABLES (QUI FAR DON)

¼ cup Chinese mushrooms   ½ teaspoon salt
   (dung goo)   ¼ cup water
1 cup Chinese celery cabbage   ¼ teaspoon sugar
   (bok choy)   dash of pepper
½ cup bamboo shoots   1½ teaspoons cornstarch
¼ cup water chestnuts   mixed with 3 tablespoons
5 eggs (don)   water

Soak mushrooms for ½ hour to soften. Drain. Shred celery cabbage, bamboo shoots and mushrooms into 1½″ x ⅛″ strips. Slice water chestnuts as thinly as possible. Deep-fry eggs for 3 minutes. Remove and place on serving dish. Using a high flame, heat a well-greased frying pan and add salt. Add celery cabbage, bamboo shoots, water chestnuts and mushrooms and stir-fry for 1 minute. Add water. Cover and cook for 2 minutes. Add sugar, pepper and cornstarch paste. Cook and stir for ½ minute. Pour over eggs.

CANTONESE EGG FOO YOUNG

3 eggs   2 tablespoons oil
¼ cup water chestnuts   ¾ teaspoon salt
1 cup Chinese celery cabbage   ⅛ pound shredded roast pork
   (bok choy)   (char shu)
½ cup bamboo shoots   ½ teaspoon sugar
¼ cup Chinese mushrooms   ½ teaspoon monosodium
   (dung goo)   glutamate

Soak mushrooms ½ hour in cold water to soften. Drain. Slice water chestnuts very thinly. Shred celery cabbage, bamboo shoots, mushrooms. Heat a frying pan very hot with 1 tablespoon oil and ¾ teaspoon salt. Add celery cabbage, bamboo shoots, water chestnuts, mushrooms and roast pork. Stir-fry for ½ minute. Cover and cook for 3½ minutes. Remove and set aside. Beat eggs. Mix vegetables, meat, sugar and monosodium glutamate. Heat pan again and add 1 tablespoon oil. Pour mixture into the pan and fry for 3 minutes on each side.

VARIATION: Cooked chicken or cooked shrimp may be substituted for roast pork.

STEAMED EGGS (JING DON)

1¼ cups water	¼ teaspoon salt
2 eggs (don)	dash of pepper
	½ teaspoon oil

Boil 2 cups of water for about three minutes. Let it cool and then measure the 1¼ cups needed. The purpose of boiling the water is to drive out the air so that the steamed eggs will be smooth. Beat eggs and add water, salt, pepper and oil. Stir lightly until the eggs are mixed with the water. Pour into a 1½″ or 2″ deep Pyrex dish. Cover and steam for about 10 minutes (jing). There is no accurate way of timing this dish, just test it as you would test custard by sticking a chopstick into the eggs to see if the inside is still liquid. Serve with generous amounts of soy sauce.

VARIATION: Add ½ cup diced roast pork (char shu) to egg mixture.

Rice and Noodle Dishes

Rice is the main staple in China although there are northern provinces that consume wheat and millet in the form of steamed bread. There are other provinces, also in the north, which prefer noodles to rice. There is a common joke among Americans eating in Chinese restaurants that one gets hungry again only one or two hours after a Chinese meal. The explanation for this is that the Americans who are used to having bread or potatoes with their meals never eat the same equivalent of rice when they are having a Chinese meal. Generally speaking an average Chinese eats from one to two full bowls of rice with each meal. Rice being the main thing to eat, the Chinese when referring to a meal will refer to "eating rice." Americans, of course, say "breaking bread."

Included in this chapter are some recipes for rice soup which the Cantonese call *jook* and the English-speaking people in the Orient call *congee*. Jook is served either for breakfast, lunch or midnight snack. It is not served in most Chinese restaurants in this country.

Noodles (mein) are very popular in the northern provinces

and are served in various forms in soup or stir-fried with vegetables and meat. Because of their great length they are served at birthdays as a symbol of longevity instead of birthday cakes, so popular here in America. Among the things which Marco Polo brought back to Italy were some noodles (mein) which the Italians re-created in various forms, the most famous of which is spaghetti. Speaking of famous noodle dishes, chow mein leads the list. Chow mein in the form in which it is served in Chinese-American restaurants in this country with the fried noodles is unknown in China. The Chinese word *chow* means fry and the word *mein* means noodles, and thus we get fried noodles, a famous Chinese dish in America, a dish considered American in China.

BOILED RICE

Measure ½ cup rice for each person. Wash rice by rinsing and rubbing between the palms of your hands until the rinsing water is clear. Drain. Add 1½ cups water for each cup of rice. Boil about five minutes until most of the visible water has been boiled off and you can see air holes on top of the rice. Cover and simmer for 20 minutes.

FRIED RICE WITH BACON, LETTUCE, TOMATOES AND ONIONS

1 cup cooked rice (fon), cooled	1 teaspoon sherry
¼ teaspoon salt	½ cup water
4 slices bacon diced	¼ teaspoon monosodium
3 leaves of lettuce diced	glutamate
1 cup diced onions	dash of pepper
2 tablespoons soy sauce	1 diced tomato

Using a high flame, heat a well-greased frying pan, and add salt. Fry bacon for about 1 minute. Add lettuce, onions, rice,

soy sauce, sherry, water, monosodium glutamate and pepper.
Cook and stir for 2 minutes. Add tomato.

ROAST PORK FRIED RICE (CHAR SHU CHOW FON)

3 cups cooked rice (fon),
   cooled
¼ teaspoon salt
1 egg
¼ cup diced roast pork
   (char shu)

¼ cup diced onions
¼ cup bean sprouts
1 teaspoon soy sauce
¼ teaspoon monosodium
   glutamate
dash of pepper

Using a high flame, heat a well-greased frying pan and add
salt. Scramble egg. Add roast pork, onions, bean sprouts and
rice. Stir-fry for 2 minutes (chow). Add soy sauce, monosodium glutamate and pepper. Cook and stir for 1 minute.

YANG CHOW FRIED RICE (YANG CHOW CHOW FON)

3 cups cooked rice (fon),
   cooled
¼ teaspoon salt
1 egg
¼ cup diced roast pork
   (char shu)
¼ cup diced boiled shrimp

⅛ cup diced boiled ham
½ cup diced lettuce
2 tablespoons finely diced
   scallions
¼ teaspoon monosodium
   glutamate
dash of pepper

Using a high flame, heat a well-greased frying pan and add
salt. Scramble egg. Add roast pork, shrimp, ham, lettuce,
scallions and rice. Stir-fry for 2 minutes (chow). Add monosodium glutamate and pepper. Cook and stir for 1 minute.

The province of Yang Chow is where fried rice originated.

SUBGUM FRIED RICE (SUBGUM CHOW FON)

3 cups cooked rice (fon),
   cooled
¼ teaspoon salt
1 egg
¼ cup diced roast pork
   (char shu)
⅛ cup diced onions
⅑ cup bean sprouts

⅛ cup diced raw
   mushrooms
⅛ cup diced green pepper
⅛ cup diced tomatoes
1 teaspoon soy sauce
¼ teaspoon monosodium
   glutamate
dash of pepper

Using a high flame, heat a well-greased frying pan and add
salt. Scramble egg. Add roast pork, onions, bean sprouts,
mushrooms, green pepper, tomatoes and rice. Stir-fry for 2
minutes. Add soy sauce, monosodium glutamate and pepper.
Cook and stir for 1 minute.

Subgum means 10 ingredients.

CHICKEN FRIED RICE (GAI CHOW FON)

3 cups cooked rice (fon),
   cooled
¼ teaspoon salt
1 egg
¼ cup diced boiled chicken
   (gai)

¼ cup diced onions
¼ cup bean sprouts
1 teaspoon soy sauce
¼ teaspoon monosodium
   glutamate
dash of pepper

Using a high flame, heat a well-greased frying pan and add
salt. Scramble egg. Add chicken, onions, bean sprouts and
rice. Stir-fry for 2 minutes (chow). Add soy sauce, monosodium glutamate and pepper. Cook and stir for 1 minute.

SHRIMP FRIED RICE (HAR CHOW FON)

3 cups cooked rice (fon)
¼ teaspoon salt
1 egg
½ cup diced boiled shrimp
  (har)

¼ cup diced onions
¼ cup bean sprouts
1 teaspoon soy sauce
¼ teaspoon monosodium
  glutamate

dash of pepper

Using a high flame, heat a well-greased frying pan and add salt. Scramble egg. Add shrimp, onion, bean sprouts and rice. Stir-fry for 2 minutes (chow). Add soy sauce, monosodium glutamate and pepper. Cook and stir for 1 minute.

CONGEE (JOOK)

¼ cup rice
2½ quarts water
⅛ pound dried scallops
  (gong yu chee) optional
  or

⅛ pound dried shrimp
  (har mei) optional

Wash rice. Add water and scallops or shrimp and bring to a boil. Simmer for 2 hours. Serves four.

PORK CHOPS COOKED WITH RICE (PORK CHOP FON)

2 pork chops
1 clove crushed garlic
½ teaspoon salt
½ cup water
1 teaspoon cornstarch mixed
  with 3 tablespoons water

1 teaspoon soy sauce
1 teaspoon sherry
dash of pepper
¼ teaspoon sugar
¼ teaspoon monosodium
  glutamate

3 cups cooked rice (fon)

Fry pork chops until done. Chop into pieces 1″ square. Using a high flame, heat a well-greased frying pan and add garlic and salt. Add pork chops, water, cornstarch paste, soy sauce, sherry, pepper, sugar and monosodium glutamate. Cook and stir for ½ minute. Mix with rice.

BEEF CONGEE (NGOW YOOK JOOK)

¼ pound ground beef (ngow yook)	¼ teaspoon salt
	¼ teaspoon sugar
1 teaspoon sherry	dash of pepper
1 teaspoon oil	1 teaspoon soy sauce
2 slices ginger root	

Make jook (p. 169). Mix all ingredients and add to jook and stir. Simmer for another 5 minutes.

FISH CONGEE (YU JOOK)

½ pound fish fillet (yu)	dash of pepper
2 tablespoons oil	1 teaspoon shredded ginger
1 teaspoon salt	root
1 teaspoon soy sauce	

Make jook (p. 169). Keep very hot. Slice fish into thin slices. Mix with other ingredients. Place jook in serving dish. Add fish and mix. Serves four.

CHICKEN CONGEE (GAI JOOK)

¼ pound boned chicken (gai)	¼ teaspoon sugar
1 teaspoon sherry	dash of pepper
1 tablespoon oil	1 teaspoon soy sauce
¼ teaspoon salt	2 slices ginger root

Make jook (p. 169). Slice chicken into 1½″ squares. Mix all ingredients and add to hot jook and stir. Simmer for another 10 minutes.

CHICKEN CHOW MEIN

2 onions
1 stalk celery
¼ pound Chinese celery
  cabbage (bok choy)
2 ounces boiled chicken meat
¼ teaspoon salt
¼ pound bean sprouts
2 cups water

2 teaspoons cornstarch mixed
  with 3 tablespoons water
½ teaspoon monosodium
  glutamate
dash of pepper
¼ teaspoon sugar
2 cups fried Chow Mein
  noodles

Slice onions, celery, celery cabbage and chicken into ½-inch slices. Using a high flame, heat a well-greased frying pan and add salt. Add onions, celery, bean sprouts and celery cabbage. Stir-fry for ½ minute. Add water. Cover and cook for 3 minutes. Add chicken, cornstarch paste, monosodium glutamate, pepper and sugar. Stir and cook for ½ minute. Put fried Chow Mein noodles in a serving dish. Pour cooked vegetables over the noodles.

For Shrimp Chow Mein, substitute 2 ounces boiled shrimp for chicken.

SUBGUM CHOW MEIN

¼ cup almonds
¼ pound boiled chicken meat
½ cup canned mushrooms
½ pound Chinese celery
  cabbage (bok choy)
¼ cup celery
1 tomato
¼ teaspoon salt or to taste
1 cup water

1½ teaspoons cornstarch
  mixed with 3 tablespoons
  water
¼ teaspoon sugar
½ teaspoon monosodium
  glutamate
dash of pepper
2 cups fried Chow Mein
  noodles

Deep-fry almonds for 3 minutes. Allow to cool. Dice chicken and all vegetables into ¼″ x ¼″ pieces. Using a high flame, heat a well-greased frying pan and add salt. Add mushrooms, celery cabbage and celery. Stir-fry for 1/2 minute. Add 1 cup water. Cover and cook for 2 minutes. Add chicken, tomato, cornstarch paste, sugar, monosodium glutamate and pepper. Cook and stir for 1/2 minute. Put fried Chow Mein noodles on a serving dish. Pour cooked vegetables over the noodles. Top with almonds.

Subgum means 10 ingredients.

ROAST PORK LO MEIN (CHAR SHU LO MEIN)

1/4 pound egg noodles (mein)
1/2 teaspoon salt
1 cup shredded Chinese celery cabbage (bok choy)
1/2 cup bean sprouts
1/4 pound shredded roast pork (char shu)

1/4 cup water
1 tablespoon oyster sauce (or soy sauce)
1 teaspoon monosodium glutamate
1/2 teaspoon sugar
dash of pepper

Bring 2 quarts of water to a full rolling boil. Boil egg noodles for 7 minutes. Drain. Using a high flame, heat a well-greased frying pan and add salt. Add celery cabbage, bean sprouts and roast pork. Stir-fry for 2 minutes. Add 1/4 cup water and place egg noodles on top of vegetables. Cover and cook for 2 minutes. Add oyster sauce, monosodium gluta-mate, sugar and pepper. Mix.

Chicken Lo Mein (Gai Lo Mein): Substitute boiled breast of chicken for roast pork.

Shrimp Lo Mein (Har Lo Mein): Substitute 1/4 pound boiled shrimp for roast pork.

Roast Duck Lo Mein (For Opp Lo Mein): Substitute 1/4 pound roast duck for roast pork.

BEEF COOKED IN RICE (BO NGOW YOOK FON)

1 cup uncooked rice (fon)	1 teaspoon oil
2 cups water	¼ teaspoon salt
¼ pound ground beef	¼ teaspoon sugar
(ngow yook)	dash of pepper
1 teaspoon sherry	1 teaspoon soy sauce

2 slices ginger root

Wash and boil the rice until all the water is boiled off. Simmer for 5 minutes. Mix all other ingredients and place on top of the rice in the pot. Cover and cook for 2 minutes (bo). Mix meat with the rice.

For Chicken Cooked In Rice (Bo Gai Fon) substitute ¼ pound sliced chicken for ground beef.

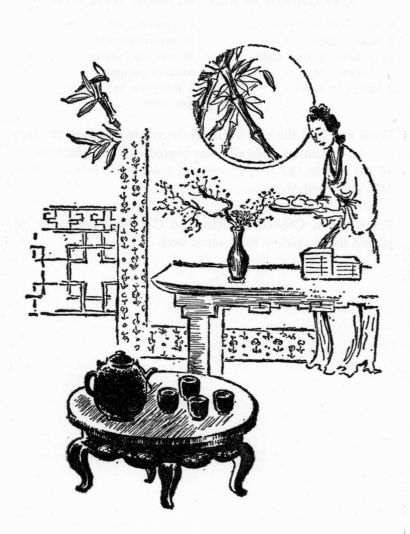

Tea

Since its discovery in the third century tea has become the national drink of China. There are many legends concerning its origin. One of the oldest attributes its discovery to Emperor Chu-Ming. During a cholera epidemic this philosopher-king discovered that if water was boiled the disease would not be contracted. He therefore ordered, on penalty of death, everyone in the kingdom to boil their water. Since boiled water is rather unpalatable the emperor, after experimenting with various herbs, discovered tea.

To Emperor Chu-Ming is attributed the first words concerning tea in Chinese literature: "Tea is better than wine for it leads not to drunkenness, neither does it cause a man to say foolish things and repent thereof in his sober moments. It is better than water for it does not carry sickness."

Another legend attributes its discovery to the great Buddhist saint, Bodhidharma, who went from India to China in the fifth century A.D. In order to convert the Chinese he vowed to contemplate the virtues of Buddha for nine years without sleep. In the sixth year he broke his vow and fell

asleep. When he awoke, in humiliation, he cut off his eye-
lids and threw them to the ground. From their blood grew a
small evergreen tree, the first tea tree on earth which forever
would prevent sleepiness.

Whatever its origin, tea was cultivated commercially in the
fifth century A.D. and became a beverage of universal popularity. Tea comes from a tree closely related to the camellia.
Since it grows on ground that will not support any other edi-
ble crop it was grown around houses, on the hillsides of rice
paddies, and high in the mountains. Tea seeds are planted in
September and are first harvested in three years. The leaves
are picked during periods of active growth called "flushes"
in April, May and August. In April picking is the finest. Also
the higher the leaves are on the tree the better the quality.
There is a belief that for tea to retain its best flavor the leaves
must be picked by feminine hands, therefore only women are
employed in this task.

Three major types of tea are produced from these leaves,
the green, oolong and black (called red in China). In black
tea the chlorophyll has been altered by fermentation before
drying; oolong is semifermented; and green tea is dried as
it is picked.

Once the leaves are dried they are curled by hand to help
release their flavor. They are then sorted according to size
and packed in metal chests. In China the size classifications
are gunpowder, young hyson, hyson, and imperial. The English classify teas (from India and Ceylon) according to size
as flowery orange pekoe, orange pekoe, and souchong. In
China tea is also sold in bricks made of compressed tea dust
for medicinal purposes.

Among the Chinese it is considered a barbarism to pollute
tea with cream and sugar. This feeling is readily understand-

able since Chinese tea has a more subtle flavor than that of other countries. Since there is a lower tanic content in Chinese tea, it is unnecessary to disguise the acid taste with dairy products.

Within the three basic varieties of tea there are many subvarieties, each with its own distinctive flavor. All come from the same genus of the three. The differences in flavor are due to the environment in which the plant grows, the time of year in which the leaves are picked and the method of preparation. Many Chinese teas are blended with dried flowers to enhance the fragrance and flavor. Among the most popular of this variety are jasmine, chrysanthemum and lei chee teas.

There is a very rare tea grown by Buddhist monks in the mountains near Amoy. Since the trees are grown on high cliffs, monkeys are trained to scale the cliffs and pick the tea leaves. Each box is labeled "monkey-plucked." This tea is sold under many Buddhist names such as Iron Kuan Yin, Iron Lo Hun or Iron Buddha. Another "monkey-plucked" tea which is more generally available is Cloud Mist from Kiangsi.

Although there is no tea ritual in China as there is in Japan, tea drinking is thoroughly embedded in Chinese social customs. Since once the tree is planted it cannot be moved without dying, it has become a symbol for fidelity. It therefore plays an important role in engagement and wedding ceremonies. Tea is one of the presents a financé sends to the girl's family when an engagement is announced. Thus when a girl is said to have accepted tea it means she is engaged. When an engagement is broken the girl is said to have split tea. At the wedding banquet, the bride must serve tea in red cups to all of the guests in strict order of their importance at the ceremony. If she should spill any tea on this occasion it is an ill omen for the marriage. As she serves the tea, each guest gives her a red envelope containing money as a token of good luck and a prosperous marriage.

Among the Chinese, tea is drunk at all times of the day. Neither a social call nor a business meeting begins without the host serving tea. In a Chinese home when it is time for a guest to leave there is no staring at clocks, yawning or embarrassed pauses in the conversation. Instead, the Chinese host when he feels the visit should end merely raises his teacup. If the guest is slow-witted or impolite, he will say, "Won't you have another cup of tea before you leave?"

Tea drinking in China has been raised to an art resembling wine tasting in France. It is said that there is a kind of tea for every season of the year and every mood. In summer green teas are raised in the mountains, and flower teas are preferred, while in winter the heavier black teas are used. Jasmine tea enhances the pleasure of reading poetry, while oolong stimulates conversation with new friends. A light green tea such as Silver Needles complements the pleasure of renewing old friendships.

Poets and philosophers have glorified this beverage with their writings. Yu Hu, a mystical poet of the Tang dynasty (618–905), wrote *Cha Ching*, the first book on the appreciation of tea. In it he wrote:

> The first cup of tea moistens my lips and throat, the second shatters my loneliness. The third causes the wrongs of life to fade gently from my recollection, and the fourth purifies my soul. The fifth lifts me to the realm of the eternal gods.

In China the cultivation of tea drinking led to the establishment of teahouses. These were social centers where people could relax, gamble, transact business or discuss art and literature over steaming cups of tea and light refreshments. There were teahouses for every social class. One of the most famous is the marble boat at the Summer Palace in Peking. It is popularly referred to as the Chinese Navy since the Dowager Empress had it built with the funds allocated for building a Chinese navy.

In recent years the Chinese in this country visit teahouses less frequently. Instead they visit small coffee shops serving American coffee and tea pastries.

The word "tea" derives from the Mandarin word *tay* which the traders adopted when they sent the first tea from the port of Amoy to England. The Russians received their first tea from Kwangtung province and adopted the Cantonese word *cha* into their language. Since a boatload of tea from China was brewed in Boston harbor, coffee has replaced tea as the national drink of the United States. According to the National Tea Institute over half the tea consumed in this country is served in Chinese restaurants. This revolution in taste can be attributed in part to political factors but also is probably due to rather uncivilized methods in brewing tea derived from the English. In strengthening tea to make it comparable to coffee the usual result is a dark red brew of diluted tanic acid. Only a people with a strong element of Puritan asceticism could find such a potion palatable.

To enjoy tea in the Chinese manner a few simple rules must be followed. It must be remembered tea is a very delicate herb. Exposure to air will cause it to lose its flavor. Therefore it must be kept in a container with a tight lid. It is at its best when freshly opened and should not be kept indefinitely.

The pot and cups should be used only for brewing tea. These implements must be thoroughly clean but never washed with soap. A low round ceramic pot should be used. A metal pot might distort the flavor, and a tall pot allows too small an area of tea leaves to be exposed to the water and the tea will not steep properly. Both the pot and cups should be scalded before the tea is brewed.

The proper amount of tea depends on the kind of tea used and must be determined by trial and error. Since the Chinese prefer a pale golden infusion with subtle flavor, only one heaping teaspoon of tea for each pot is used in brewing most popular teas. The water should be freshly drawn and poured on the tea leaves just at the moment it reaches a rolling boil. Boiling for a longer time will drive too much oxygen out of the water and the tea will have a flat taste. The tea should steep from 3 to 5 minutes.

Once the first pot of tea is drunk add a few new leaves and brew a second pot. Experts consider the second infusion to be superior to the first.

While it is impossible to list every variety of Chinese teas, I have composed a list of the most popular of them. At present some of these are in short supply but those starred are generally available. With each tea is listed a pastime which the tea will enhance, according to custom.

NAME	PROVINCE	TYPE	SERVED
Black Dragon	Canton	Black	Served with the evening meal
Clear Distance	Canton	Black	For late at night
*Chrysanthe-mum	Chekiang	Dragon Well and Flowers	Mix with rock candy and drink with Chinese pastry after meals
Cloud Mist	Kiangsi	Green	Serve in afternoon or teatime
Dragon Beard	Canton	Green	Pastime drink, afternoon, listening to music
*Dragon Well	Chinkiang	Green	Among the finest green teas, serve day and night
*Eyebrows of Longevity	Canton	Green	Serve in the garden on a spring afternoon

NAME	PROVINCE	TYPE	SERVED
Fragrant Petals	Chinkiang	Green	Serve at home when entertaining relatives or close friends
*Hung Cha	Fukien	Black	Tea served at the Boston Tea Party. Most common at teahouses in China, restaurants in America
Iron Kuan Yin	Fukien	Black ⎫	Served as fine brandy. Produced by Buddhist monks
Iron Lo Han	Fukien	Black ⎭	
*Jasmine	Taiwan	Oolong and Flowers	For reading poetry with your love
*Keemun	Kiangsu	Black	Playing chess
*Lo Cha	Taiwan	Oolong	Conversation
*Lychee	Taiwan	Oolong and Lychee Flowers	Served to renew friendship
Ning Chow	Canton	Black	To begin the day, before breakfast
*Silver Needle	Canton	Green	Ideal for banquets
Su Tang	Fukien	Black	For a winter evening
Water Nymph	Canton	Green	Light tea, midmorning
Woo Lung	Chekiang	Black	Most popular at public teahouses, with talk of the day
Wu-I	Yunan	Black	To cure a cold

Index